There is NO LIMIT to what God can do through us, with us, and in us when we truly surrender and let Him be GOD!

Peace & Joy for the Incredible Journey!

Bless You!

O·

LIN

Author of the *New York Times* and international bestseller *Unstoppable*

NICK VUJICIC

LIMITLESS

Devotions for a Ridiculously Good Life

WATERBROOK
PRESS

Limitless
Published by WaterBrook Press
12265 Oracle Boulevard, Suite 200
Colorado Springs, Colorado 80921

Details in some anecdotes and stories have been changed to protect the identities of the persons involved.

Hardcover ISBN 978-0-307-73091-6
eBook ISBN 978-0-307-73092-3

Material in *Limitless* is excerpted from *Life Without Limits* and *Unstoppable* by Nick Vujicic.

Cover design by Kristopher K. Orr; cover photography by Mike Heath, Magnus Creative; cover background image by Masterfile

Published in the United States by WaterBrook Multnomah, an imprint of the Crown Publishing Group, a division of Random House Inc., New York.

WaterBrook and its deer colophon are registered trademarks of Random House Inc.

Library of Congress Cataloging-in-Publication Data
Vujicic, Nick.
    Limitless devotions for a ridiculously good life / Nick Vujicic. — 1st ed.
      p. cm.
    ISBN 978-0-307-73091-6 — ISBN 978-0-307-73092-3 (electronic)
  1. Christian life—Meditations. 2. Consolation. I. Title.
    BV4501.3.V855 2013
    242—dc23

                                                    2012037878

Printed in the United States of America
2013 — First Edition

10 9 8 7 6 5 4 3 2 1

Special Sales
Most WaterBrook Multnomah books are available at special quantity discounts when purchased in bulk by corporations, organizations, and special-interest groups. Custom imprinting or excerpting can also be done to fit special needs. For information, please e-mail SpecialMarkets@WaterBrookMultnomah.com or call 1-800-603-7051.

CONTENTS

Introduction

Hello and welcome to my first Christian devotional. This book draws on material from two of my previous books, *Life Without Limits* and *Unstoppable.* It is intended to provide you with a series of quick inspirational and faith-building stories to be read daily or whenever you feel you need them. There are no rules other than God's.

I do want to comment on the title, *Limitless,* which refers not to my abilities or your abilities but to God's limitless love and power. As you may already know from my speeches, books, and videos—or you may suspect from photographs—I am technically more limited physically than most people.

I was born without arms or legs. Though I lacked limbs, I was blessed with a loving and supportive family that includes not just my parents and my brother and sister (both of whom came fully equipped) but also many cousins, aunts, and uncles. Even better, I was given the gift of Christian faith.

That's not to say I did not struggle with my faith, especially when I reached those difficult adolescent years when we all try to figure out our place in the world—where we fit in and what we have to contribute. I prayed to God that I would wake up with arms and legs. Those prayers were not answered. I grew angry and then depressed. Thoughts of suicide drove me to make an attempt on my own life, but I stopped short when I realized my death would burden my loved ones with guilt and grief.

Over time, I came to understand that God had not brought me into the world without limbs to punish me. Instead, He had a plan for me, an incredible plan to serve Him by inspiring and leading others to lives of Christian faith.

If God can take someone like me, someone without arms and legs, and use me as His hands and feet, He can use anybody. It's not about ability. The only thing God needs from you is a willing heart.

What do you need to live in faith on this earth and then to be blessed with eternal life in the kingdom of heaven? You need a relationship with Jesus Christ as your personal savior. Where you are weak, God is strong. When you walk in faith each and every day, your life has no limits.

You can take that on faith, which I highly recommend, or you can take it from the pages that follow, which offer my life as testimony to the incredible power of the Lord our God. I am a man who is not disabled but enabled. I travel the world on God's business, reaching out to believers and sinners, rich and poor. I'm allowed to deliver my messages of faith, hope, and love in nations where many Christians fear to tread.

I have a ridiculously good life, and now since my marriage in 2012, I have the honor and the joy of sharing it with a strong Christian wife who is as beautiful on the inside as she is on the outside. In my days of despair, one of my most depressing thoughts was that no woman could ever love a man without arms or legs. I was so, so wrong. My vision was limited. I forgot that ours is a loving God, wise in ways that we cannot comprehend.

Like me, you may not be able to see or even imagine what He has in store for you. My goal with this devotional is to help you expand your vision and build your faith by sharing what God has done for me and for the special men, women, and children I've met in my travels around the world.

I hope you enjoy the devotions and you benefit from them. But more important, I hope they help you get on the right track with God so that you are transformed with Him and come to trust that, through Him, all things are possible.

1 Free from Limitations

> When I was beleaguered and bitter,
>> totally consumed by envy,
> I was totally ignorant, a dumb ox
>> in your very presence.
> I'm still in your presence,
>> but you've taken my hand.
> You wisely and tenderly lead me,
>> and then you bless me.
> You're all I want in heaven!
>> You're all I want on earth!

PSALM 73:21–25, MSG

A question I'm often asked is, "Nick, how can you be so happy?" I'll give you the short answer: I found happiness when I realized that as imperfect as I may be, I am the perfect Nick Vujicic. I am God's creation, designed according to His plan for me. That's not to say that there isn't room for improvement.

I'm always trying to be better so I can better serve Him and the world!

I believe my life has no limits. I want you to feel the same way about your life, no matter what your challenges may be. As we begin our journey together, please take a moment to think about any limitations you've placed on your life or that you've allowed others to place on it. Now think about what it would be like to be free of those limitations. What would your life be if *anything* were possible?

I'm officially *disabled,* but I'm truly *enabled* because of my lack of limbs. My unique challenges have opened up remarkable opportunities to reach so many in need. You have your own challenges, and you, too, are imperfect. But you are the perfect YOU!

Too often we tell ourselves we aren't smart enough or attractive enough or talented enough to pursue our dreams. We buy into what others say about us, or we put restrictions on ourselves. What's worse is that when we consider ourselves unworthy, we are putting limits on how *God* can work through us!

When you give up on your dreams, you put God in a box. After all, you are His creation. He made you for a purpose. Therefore your life cannot be limited any more than God's love can be contained. Just imagine what is possible for you!

LIMITLESS *Life*

I have a choice. You have a choice. We can choose to dwell on disappointments and short-comings. We can choose to be bitter, angry, or sad. Or when faced with hard times and hurtful people, we can choose to learn from the experience and move forward, taking responsibility for our own happiness. Think about how you want to respond the next time a challenge comes your way.

2 Just Stay in the Game

Bow down Your ear, O LORD, hear me;
For I am poor and needy.
Preserve my life, for I am holy;
You are my God;
Save Your servant who trusts in You!
Be merciful to me, O Lord,
For I cry to You all day long.
Rejoice the soul of Your servant,
For to You, O Lord, I lift up my soul.
For You, Lord, are good, and ready
      to forgive,
And abundant in mercy to all those
      who call upon You.

PSALM 86:1–5

I have discovered time and again that when we ask for God's
help and then take action, knowing in our hearts that He is

watching over us, there is no reason to be fearful. My parents taught me this mostly in the way they lived each day. They are the greatest examples of faith in action I have witnessed.

Although I arrived on this earth missing, as my mother says, "a few bits and pieces," I am blessed in many, many ways. My parents have always been there for me. They did not coddle me. They disciplined me when I needed it and gave me room to make my own mistakes. Most of all, they are wonderful role models.

I was their first child and definitely a surprise package. Despite doing all the usual maternity tests, my mother's doctor detected no indication that I would come into the world with neither arms nor legs. My mother was an experienced nurse who had assisted in hundreds of deliveries, so she took all the precautions during her pregnancy.

Needless to say, she and my father were quite stunned that I arrived without limbs. Like all babies, I did not come with an instruction book, but my parents sure would have welcomed a little guidance. They knew of no other parents who had raised a child without limbs in a world designed for people with a complete set.

They were distraught at first, as any parents would be. Anger, guilt, fear, depression, despair—their emotions ran away with them for the first week or so. Many tears were shed. They grieved for the perfectly formed child they had envisioned but did not receive. They grieved, too, because they feared that my life would be very difficult.

My parents could not imagine what plan God had in mind for such a boy. Yet once they'd recovered from their initial shock, they decided to put their trust in God. They gave up their attempts to understand why God had given them such a child. Instead, they surrendered to His plan, whatever it might be, and then they went about raising me as best they could, the only way they could—pouring into me all of their love one day at a time. I could never ask for anything better than that. As a result of their love and encouragement, I am not afraid to try anything.

LIMITLESS *Life* _____

Life may be kicking you around right now. You may wonder if your fortunes will improve. I'm telling you that you can't even imagine the good that awaits you if you refuse to give up. Stay focused on your dream. Do whatever it takes to stay in the chase. You have the power to change your circumstances. Go after whatever it is you desire.

3 Posttraumatic Growth

My brethren, count it all joy when you fall into various trials, knowing that the testing of your faith produces patience. But let patience have its perfect work, that you may be perfect and complete, lacking nothing. If any of you lacks wisdom, let him ask of God, who gives to all liberally and without reproach, and it will be given to him. But let him ask in faith, with no doubting.

JAMES 1:2–6

I have always believed that God puts us through challenges to strengthen us. In recent years, researchers in health psychology have found support for this in studies of people who have experienced severe stress and trauma across a wide range—from serious and life-threatening illnesses to catastrophic events to the loss of a loved one. While you often hear about people's struggles with posttraumatic stress, psychologists have also found that those who deal successfully with health challenges can experience posttraumatic or adversarial *growth*.

Researchers found that many who successfully deal with physical adversity actually grow in positive ways, including these:

- They realize they are stronger than they thought, and they tend to recover more quickly from future challenges.
- They discover who truly cares about them, and those relationships grow stronger.
- They put greater value on each day and on the good things in their lives.
- They become stronger spiritually.

I believe there is yet another benefit that can come of major disabilities and health challenges. I think God allows some of us to be afflicted so that that we can comfort others just as God has comforted us. This explanation in particular makes sense to me because I have experienced the truth of it time after time after time.

I don't claim to always understand God's plan. I do know that heaven will not be like this temporary life. But it can be difficult to have certainty when God does something that seems harsh or unfair. You have to take comfort and strength from Him. You can make the decision to give the situation to God by putting in a request for His help.

Now, it may be impossible not to be anxious when dealing with illness, disabilities, or other life-threatening challenges, but you can find peace by putting things in God's hands. He can give you strength one day at a time, whether you need it for your own challenges or because you are grieving for someone else.

Know that whatever happens, there is no sickness or disease or death in the next life, but there has to be an end to us all on earth. His plan is not to keep us here to suffer and die. God wants us to be with Him in heaven forever.

Still, while we are here in our temporary lives, we have a beautiful opportunity to know God and to share His love with others who do not yet know that Jesus Christ died for their sins. While eternal life in heaven will be great, having a relationship with God while we are on earth is a tremendous opportunity here.

LIMITLESS *Life*

Whatever circumstances you face, God will use you for His purposes. It may be years before you understand what that purpose might be. In some cases, you may never know the full extent of His plans or why He allows some things to happen to you. That's why it is necessary to put your faith in action by knowing God is with you and by knowing that even though bad things may happen, they do not change the fact that He loves you.

4 Serenity of Surrender

> Be anxious for nothing, but in everything by
> prayer and supplication, with thanksgiving,
> let your requests be made known to God;
> and the peace of God, which surpasses all
> understanding, will guard your hearts and
> minds through Christ Jesus.
>
> PHILIPPIANS 4:6–7

Our lives on this earth are not about what *we* want. You and I were created and placed in the natural world because of what God wants for us. He sent His Son here to die for our sins, and Jesus made the ultimate surrender to follow His Father's plan to give us the gift of eternal life. There is an incredible peace in surrendering our lives to Him just as Jesus did.

That peace can be yours when you surrender your fears and the need to control your life, as well as any need to know the outcome of your actions. You put it all in God's hands and commit to follow His will. When you are searching for God's will in your life, whether it's trying to make decisions or looking for opportunities, you can't always expect a sign from God. Those are rare and wonderful occasions. What I've come to look for instead is a *sense of peace.*

If serenity remains in my heart as I pray and move forward with a decision to act on an opportunity, I feel like I'm following His will. If I lose that sense of peace at any point, I stop, pray some more, and reconsider. I believe if I'm headed the wrong way, God will change my heart and guide me.

Everyone has a process. Some people may have many friends who advise them, or maybe they base their decisions on the alignment of the stars or a gut feeling. My process is surrender. God understands us to the core because He created us. He feels what we feel, but His vision reaches those places we cannot see. There are many people I look to for advice and wisdom, but there is no one in God's league when it comes to guidance. I'm grateful to have opportunities, and often it seems like I'm walking down the corridor of a giant hotel with hundreds of doors waiting to be opened. It's difficult to know which doors are right for me, but through my surrender, patience, and trust in Him, God guides me.

Of course, God may say no to your plan one day, but the next He may say yes to something even better. You don't know what God can do with your life until you give it to Him and feel the bliss in your relationship with Him. Whenever I become anxious about achieving *my* goals, I find peace knowing that I am here because God loves me and that He will be there when I let go.

LIMITLESS *Life*

There is nothing quite as soothing as accepting that you don't have to work it all out because God will. You can surrender yourself to Him and then wait patiently. Through Him, everything is possible. Is there a big decision or something else weighing you down right now? Try surrendering it to God and letting Him guide your heart as you move forward.

 Keep Moving

> "For I know the plans I have for you,"
> declares the LORD, "plans to prosper you
> and not to harm you, plans to give you
> hope and a future."
>
> JEREMIAH 29:11, NIV

As God's child, you are beautiful and precious, worth more than all the diamonds in the world. You and I are perfectly suited to be who we were meant to be! Still, it should always be our goal to become an even better person and stretch our boundaries by dreaming big. Adjustments are necessary along the way because life isn't always rosy, but it is always worth living. I'm here to tell you that no matter what your circumstances may be, as long as you are breathing, you have a contribution to make.

Life can seem cruel, no doubt about it. Sometimes the bad

breaks pile up, and you just can't see a way out. The fact is that, as mere mortals, you and I have limited vision. We can't possibly see what lies ahead. That's both the bad news and the good news. My encouragement to you is that what lies ahead may be far better than anything you ever thought possible. But it's up to you to get over it, get up, and show up!

Whether your life is good and you want to make it better, or whether it's so bad you just want to stay in bed, the fact is that what happens from this very moment on is up to you and your Maker. True, you cannot control everything. Too often bad stuff happens to people no matter how good they are. It may not be fair that you weren't born into a life of ease, but if that is your reality, you have to work with it.

You may stumble. Others may doubt you. When I focused on public speaking as a career path, even my parents questioned my decision. "Don't you think that an accounting career, with your own practice, would be more appropriate for your circumstances and provide a better future?" my dad asked.

Yes, from most perspectives a career in accounting probably made more sense for me because I do have a talent for number crunching. But from an early age I've had this absolute passion for sharing my faith and my hope of a better life.

When you find your true purpose, passion follows. You absolutely live to pursue it.

LIMITLESS *Life*

If you are still searching for your path in life, know that it's okay to feel a little frustration. This is a marathon, not a sprint. Your yearning for more meaning is a sign that you are growing, moving beyond limitations, and developing your talents. It's healthy to look at where you are from time to time and to consider whether your actions and priorities are serving your highest purpose.

𝒪 Finding True Reward

> Whatever my eyes desired I did not keep
>   from them.
> I did not withhold my heart from any
>   pleasure,
> For my heart rejoiced in all my labor;
> And this was my reward from all my labor.
> Then I looked on all the works that my
>   hands had done
> And on the labor in which I had toiled;
> And indeed all was vanity and grasping
>   for the wind.
> There was no profit under the sun.
>
> ECCLESIASTES 2:10–11

Helen Keller lost her sight and hearing due to an illness before she was two years old, but she went on to become a world-renowned author, speaker, and social activist. This great woman said true happiness comes through "fidelity to a wor-thy purpose."

What does that mean? For me, it means being faithful to your gifts, growing them, sharing them, and taking joy in them. It means moving beyond the pursuit of self-satisfaction to the more mature search for meaning and fulfillment.

The greatest rewards come when you give something of yourself. It's about bettering the lives of others, being a part of something bigger than you, and making a positive difference. You don't have to be Mother Teresa to do that. You can even be a "disabled" guy and make an impact.

Your own search for meaning and fulfillment may still be under way. But I don't think you can really feel fulfilled with-out serving others. Each of us hopes to put our talents and knowledge to use for some benefit beyond just paying the bills.

In today's world, even though we may be fully conscious of the spiritual emptiness of material attainment, we still need reminders that fulfillment has nothing to do with having pos-sessions. People certainly try the strangest methods for attain-ing fulfillment. They may drink a six-pack of beer. They may drug themselves into oblivion. They may alter their bodies to achieve some arbitrary standard of beauty. They may work their whole lives to reach the pinnacle of success, only to have it mercilessly yanked from them in the next second.

But most sensible people know there are no easy routes to

long-term happiness. If you place your bets on temporary plea-sures, you will find only temporary satisfaction. With cheap thrills, you get what you pay for—here today, gone tomorrow.

Life isn't about having; it's about being. You could sur-round yourself with all that money can buy, and you still might be as miserable as a human can be. I know people with perfect bodies who don't have half the happiness I've found.

LIMITLESS *Life*

You'll find contentment when your talents and passion are completely engaged and in full force. Recognize instant self-gratification for what it is. Resist the temptation to grab for material objects like the perfect house, the coolest clothes, or the hottest car. The "if I just had X, I would be happy" syndrome is a mass delusion. When you look for happiness in mere objects, they are never enough. Look around. Look within.

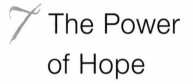7 The Power of Hope

O God, do not be far from me;
O my God, make haste to help me!
Let them be confounded and consumed
Who are adversaries of my life;
Let them be covered with reproach
        and dishonor
Who seek my hurt.

But I will hope continually,
And will praise You yet more and more.
My mouth shall tell of Your righteousness
And Your salvation all the day,
For I do not know their limits.
I will go in the strength of the Lord GOD;
I will make mention of Your righteousness,
        of Yours only.

PSALM 71:12–16

Time and again in my life and in my travels I have witnessed the incredible power of the human spirit. I know for certain that miracles happen, but only for those who hang on to hope. What is hope? It is where dreams begin. It is the voice of your purpose. It speaks to you and reassures you that whatever happens to you doesn't live within you. You may not be able to control what happens to you, but you can control how you respond.

My belief in the power of hope over despair was reinforced in 2008 during my first visit to China. I saw the Great Wall and marveled at the grandeur of one of the world's most incredible wonders. But the most powerful moment of this trip came when I saw the joyful glimmer in the eyes of a young Chinese girl. She was performing with other children who had put together a show worthy of an Olympic spectacle. This girl's jubilant expression caught my attention, and I could not look away. While she moved in precision with the other dancers, she simultaneously balanced a spinning plate overhead. She was concentrating so, so hard, yet despite everything she had to think about, she still had this look of intense happiness that moved me to tears.

You see, this girl and all the children in the show were among more than four thousand young people orphaned by a massive earthquake that had hit the region just a few months earlier. My caregiver, our travel coordinator, and I had come to this orphanage with supplies for them, and I'd been asked to speak to them to raise their spirits.

As we traveled to the orphanage, I was overwhelmed by the damage and suffering that had been caused by the earthquake. In the face of such devastation, I worried that I would not know what to tell these orphans. The earth had opened up and swallowed everything they had loved and known. I had never endured anything so terrible. What could I say to them? We had brought warm coats and other clothing for them, but how could I give them hope?

When I arrived at the orphanage, I was mobbed. One child after another embraced me. I didn't speak their language, but that didn't matter. Their faces said it all. Despite their circumstances, they were radiant. I should not have worried about what words to say to help them. I didn't have to inspire these children. Instead, they inspired me with their courageous, soaring spirits. They had lost their parents, their homes, and all their belongings, yet they were expressing joy.

LIMITLESS *Life*

Hope appears even in the worst of times to give us proof of God's presence. Keep looking forward, dare to wish for a better life, and pursue your dreams with all your power.

8 Beauty Isn't What Is Seen

Charm is deceitful and beauty is passing,
But a woman who fears the LORD, she
      shall be praised.
Give her of the fruit of her hands,
And let her own works praise her in
      the gates.

PROVERBS 31:30–31

The kind of self-love and self-acceptance I advocate is not about loving yourself in a self-absorbed, conceited way. The self-love I encourage is self-*less*. You give more than you take. You offer without being asked. You share when you don't have much. You find happiness by making others smile. You love yourself because you are not all about yourself. You are happy with who you are because you make others happy to be around you.

If your self-love goes too far in the direction of self-absorption, it becomes vanity. Vanity is laughable, because just as soon as you think you are looking good and sexy and worthy of the cover of *People* magazine, along comes a life lesson to make you realize that beauty really is in the eyes of the beholder, and what is on the outside is not nearly as important as what is on the inside.

Recently I met a blind Australian girl. We were doing a fun run to raise money to provide medical equipment for needy kids. She was about five years old. Her mum introduced her to me after the event. The mother explained to her that I had been born with no arms and no legs.

Blind people sometimes ask to touch my body so they can comprehend what someone without limbs is like. I don't mind it, so when the girl asked her mother if she could "see" for herself, I gave permission. Her mum guided her hand over my shoulders and over my little left foot. The girl's reaction was interesting. She was very calm as she felt my empty shoulder sockets and my strange little foot. Then, when she put her hands on my face, she screamed!

It was hilarious.

"What? My beautiful face scares you?" I asked, laughing.

"No! It's that hair all over you! Are you a wolf?"

She had never felt a beard before. When she touched my stubble, she freaked out. She told her mother that it was sad I was so hairy! This girl had her own idea of what was attractive, and obviously my beard was not on the list. I wasn't offended. I was glad to be reminded that beauty is definitely in the eyes—and touch—of the beholder.

LIMITLESS *Life*

Love yourself as God loves you—for what is on the inside. Let that inner love and self-acceptance spill to the outside. You will radiate good feelings that others can actually perceive!

9 Hope for the Impossible

Therefore, having been justified by faith, we have peace with God through our Lord Jesus Christ, through whom also we have access by faith into this grace in which we stand, and rejoice in hope of the glory of God. And not only that, but we also glory in tribulations, knowing that tribulation produces perseverance; and perseverance, character; and character, hope. Now hope does not disappoint, because the love of God has been poured out in our hearts by the Holy Spirit who was given to us.

ROMANS 5:1–5

People around the world were deeply saddened by the devastating 2010 earthquake in Haiti. Yet for all the tragedies that came with this massive disaster, the horrific circumstances also brought out the survivors' best qualities, such as refusing to surrender despite the overwhelming odds stacked against them.

Marie's son Emmanuel was thought to be among the dead buried under a building. The twenty-one-year-old tailor had been with his mother in her apartment when the earthquake hit. She escaped, but she could not find him afterward. Their building now was just a heap of rubble. Marie looked for her son at an emergency camp set up for people who had lost their homes, but she could not find him among the other survivors. She waited, hoping he still might make his way there.

After several days, she went back through the chaos and the destruction to search for her son. Heavy machinery at work on the site made it difficult to hear, but at one point Marie thought she heard Emmanuel calling for her.

"At that moment," she told a reporter, "I knew it was possible to save him."

Marie let everyone know that her son had called to her from under the rubble, but no one was able to help her. When some groups of international rescue workers arrived, she was able to find an experienced team of engineers. She convinced them her son was still alive. Using their equipment and knowledge, they cut through steel, concrete, and debris at exactly the spot where she had heard her son's voice.

They dug until they uncovered Emmanuel's hand, reaching out to them. They continued until they freed his shoulder and they were able to pull him out. He had been buried for ten days. He was severely dehydrated, covered in dust, and very hungry, but he survived.

Sometimes all you will have is your belief that something is possible, that miracles can happen. As it was for Marie, the world around you may be in chaos, but you should not give in to despair. Instead, believe that God will provide whatever you lack! That belief spurred Marie to action. Her actions brought her within the sound of her son's voice. It's not a stretch to recognize that Marie's hope kept Emmanuel alive, is it?

LIMITLESS *Life* _____

> Life may not be going well for you now, but as long as you are here, as long as you press forward, anything is possible. Hold on to hope.

10 Prepare for the Best

Therefore we do not lose heart. Even though our outward man is perishing, yet the inward man is being renewed day by day. For our light affliction, which is but for a moment, is working for us a far more exceeding and eternal weight of glory, while we do not look at the things which are seen, but at the things which are not seen. For the things which are seen are temporary, but the things which are not seen are eternal.

2 CORINTHIANS 4:16–18

You may be skeptical that anything is possible by hanging on to hope. Or perhaps you have been brought down so low that finding the strength to crawl out of your despair seems impossible. There was a time when I felt exactly that way. I was absolutely convinced that my life would never be of value and that I would only be a burden to those I loved.

My parents were not prepared for a child without limbs when I was born, and they were despondent as a result. Who could blame them? Every mother and father tries to envision the future for the children they bring into the world. My parents had difficulty projecting what sort of future I would have, and as I grew older, so did I.

We all have at times seen our vision for our lives crash into a cruel reality like a speeding car into a brick wall. The particulars of your experience may be unique, but situations of despair are all too human. Teens often e-mail me stories of abuse and neglect ripping apart their families. Adults share stories in which drugs or alcohol or pornography have left them crippled. Some days it seems like half the people I talk to are dealing with cancer or some other life-threatening medical condition.

How do you stay hopeful in such situations? You trust in God, remember that you are here for a reason, and dedicate yourself to fulfilling that purpose. Whatever challenge you are facing, you are blessed in ways that will help you find a way through it. Just think of my parents and of the hopelessness they once faced.

Martin Luther King Jr. said, "Everything that is done in the world is done by hope." I know for certain that as long as you draw breath, hope is available to you. You and I are only human. We cannot see into the future. Instead, we picture the possibilities for what might be. Only God knows how our lives will unfold. Hope is His gift to us, a window to look through.

LIMITLESS *Life*

> Trust in Him, keep hope in your heart, and even when faced with the worst, do whatever you can to prepare yourself for the best! We cannot know the future He has planned for us.

11 No Comparison

> The thief does not come except to steal, and
> to kill, and to destroy. I have come that they
> may have life, and that they may have it
> more abundantly.
>
> JOHN 10:10

Since I had been born without arms or legs, I never missed
them. I found ways to do most tasks on my own. I had a happy
childhood of skateboarding, fishing, and playing "room soccer" with my brother and sister and many cousins. Most of the
time, I didn't mind the favorable attention my unusual body
brought. Sometimes even good things came of it. Australian
newspapers and television stations did features on me, lauding
my determined efforts to live without limits.

Bullying and hurtful remarks were rare until I reached an
age when nearly all kids are subjected to similar torment on the
playground, in the cafeteria, or on the bus. My self-destructive

urges came when I lost faith and focused on what I could not do rather than on what I could do. I lost hope in the future because I limited my vision to what I could see instead of opening myself to what was possible—and even to some things that seemed impossible.

No one should feel sorry for me or play down their own challenges by comparing them to mine. We all have problems and concerns. Comparing yours to mine may be helpful, but the real perspective you should adopt is that God is bigger than any problems any of us might have. I'm grateful that other people find a fresh and more positive perspective on their lives by looking at mine for inspiration, but that is not what I'm all about.

Although I lack a few items on the standard limb package, I'm having a ridiculously good life. In fact, my youthful self-acceptance and self-confidence did not begin to crumble until I began relentlessly comparing myself to my peers. Then, instead of taking pride in what I could do, I dwelled on those things my mates could do that were beyond my abilities. Instead of seeing myself as enabled, I saw myself as disabled. Instead of taking pride in my uniqueness, I yearned to be what I was not. My focus shifted. I felt worthless. I saw myself as a burden on my family. My future seemed without hope.

Negative thoughts and emotions can overwhelm you and rob you of perspective. If you don't shut them down, self-destruction can seem like the only escape because you can't see another way out.

A great many people have fleeting thoughts of suicide or self-harm. What will save your life in these situations is to shift your perspective from yourself to those you love, from the pain of right now to the greater possibilities of the future.

LIMITLESS *Life*

> When self-destructive and suicidal thoughts torment you, I recommend putting faith in action, whether it is a faith that you will have better days and a better life, or faith that those who love you, including your Creator, will help you through this storm.

12 Triumph over Tragedy

Lord, how long will You look on?
Rescue me from their destructions,
My precious life from the lions.
I will give You thanks in the great assembly;
I will praise You among many people.

PSALM 35:17–18

You may recall that world-class surfer Bethany Hamilton lost her left arm at the age of thirteen when she was attacked by a tiger shark in Hawaii. Prior to the shark attack, Bethany was well-known among surfers, but after she survived that tragedy and returned to her sport, praising God and thanking Him for His blessings, she became admired internationally for her courageous spirit and amazing faith. Now she travels the globe to inspire people and to share her beliefs.

Her goal is "just to tell about my faith in God and to let everyone know that He loves them and to explain just how much He took care of me that day. I shouldn't be here, because I lost seventy percent of my blood that morning."

I had not previously realized how close Bethany came to dying. She told me how she prayed as they rushed her to a hospital forty-five minutes away and how her paramedic whispered encouraging words of faith: "God will never leave you nor forsake you."

Things were looking grim. When they arrived at the hospital and hurriedly prepped her for surgery, they found that all of the operating rooms were being used. Bethany was fading fast. But one patient gave up his knee surgery, which was just about to begin, so his doctor could operate on Bethany. The patient? Bethany's own dad!

Amazing, isn't it? The surgeon was prepped and ready, so they just switched daughter for dad and went to work, saving her life.

Being so healthy and athletic and having such a positive attitude, Bethany bounced back faster than her doctors expected. She was surfing again just three weeks after the attack.

Bethany said her faith in God led her to conclude that losing her arm was part of His plan for her life. Instead of feeling sorry for herself, she accepted it. In her first competition against many of the world's best female surfers, she finished third—with only one arm! She says that the loss of her arm is a blessing in many ways, because now, whenever she does well in a competition, it inspires other people that their lives have no limits!

"God has definitely answered my prayer to use me. He speaks to people when they hear my story," she says. "People tell me that they have drawn closer to God, started to believe in God, found hope for their lives, or were inspired to overcome a difficult circumstance. I just praise God when I hear that because it's not me doing anything for them—God is the One who is helping them. I'm so stoked that God would let me be a part of His plan."

LIMITLESS *Life*

Few would have blamed Bethany if she had quit surfing altogether after the shark attack. She had to learn how to balance on a surfboard all over again, but that didn't faze her. She trusted that even though something terrible had happened to her, good could come of it. The same is true for you!

13 Proof Not Required

> Now faith is being sure of what we hope for
> and certain of what we do not see. This is
> what the ancients were commended for.
>
> By faith we understand that the universe
> was formed at God's command, so that what
> is seen was not made out of what was visible.
>
> HEBREWS 11:1–3, NIV

You and I cannot see what God has in store for us. That is why you should never believe that your worst fears are your fate or that you will never rise again when you are down. You must have faith in yourself, in your purpose, and in God's plan for your life. Then, you must put fears and insecurities aside and trust that you will find your way. You may not have a clue as to what lies ahead, but it's better to act on life than simply let life act on you.

If you have faith, you don't need proof. You live it. You don't need to have all the right answers, just the right questions. No one knows what the future holds. Most of the time, God's plan is beyond our grasp, beyond even the reach of our imaginations. As a ten-year-old boy I never would have believed that within the next ten years God would send me all over the world to speak to millions of people, inspiring them and leading them to Jesus Christ. Nor could I ever have known that the love of my family would one day be matched and even surpassed by the love of the intelligent, faith-filled, fearless, and beautiful woman who became my wife. That boy who despaired at the thought of his future is at peace today as a man.

I know who I am, and I take one step at a time, knowing God is on my side. My life is overflowing with purpose and love. Are my days worry free? Is every day blessed with sunshine and flowers? No. We all know life doesn't work that way. But I thank God for each and every moment that He allows me to walk the path He has set out for me. You and I are here for a purpose. I've found mine, and you should take my story as an assurance that your path awaits you too.

LIMITLESS *Life* _____

> If you have faith, you will find, as I have, that God's vision for your life is far greater than anything you might imagine. God doesn't make mistakes!

 Never Be
Without Hope

The LORD kills and makes alive;
He brings down to the grave and brings up.
The LORD makes poor and makes rich;
He brings low and lifts up.
He raises the poor from the dust
And lifts the beggar from the ash heap,
To set them among princes
And make them inherit the throne of glory.

1 SAMUEL 2:6–8

I've seen people's amazing capacity to rise above their circumstances in such bleak places as orphanages in China, the slums of Mumbai, and the prisons of Romania. I once spoke at a social welfare center in South Korea where some of the residents were disabled and others were single mothers. The power of their spirits amazed me. I visited a prison in South Africa with concrete walls and rusted bars. The worst criminals were not allowed in our chapel service, but I could hear many of them outside, throughout the prison, singing along with the gospel music. It was as if the Holy Spirit had filled the entire population with God's joy. They were captive on the outside but free on the inside because of their faith and hope. Walking out the prison gates that day, I felt that those inmates seemed freer than many of those outside the prison.

Remember, sadness serves a purpose. It is perfectly natural to experience this emotion, but you should never let it dominate your thoughts day and night. You can control your response by turning to more positive thoughts and actions that lift your spirits.

Because I am a spiritual person, I look to my faith in sorrowful times. Surprisingly, it is my training in accounting that offers a more pragmatic approach. If you say you are without hope, that means you believe there is a zero chance of anything good happening in your life ever again.

Zero? That's pretty extreme, don't you think? The power of believing in better days is so indisputable to me that it seems far more probable that your days will change for the better. Hope, along with faith and love, is one of the pillars of spirituality. Whatever your beliefs, you should never be without hope, because everything good in life begins with it. If you didn't have hope, would you ever plan to start a family? Without hope, would you ever try to learn something new? Hope is the springboard for nearly every step we take.

Isaiah 40:31 says, "Those who hope in the LORD will renew their strength. They will soar on wings like eagles; they will run and not grow weary, they will walk and not be faint" (NIV). The first time I heard this passage, I realized I didn't need arms and legs. Don't ever forget that God never gives up on you.

LIMITLESS *Life*

> You, too, can allow hope to live in your heart.
> Have the courage to pursue your dreams and
> never doubt your ability to meet whatever
> challenges come your way. Keep moving ahead,
> because action creates momentum, which in
> turn creates unanticipated opportunities.

# Enjoy the Ride

The wilderness and the wasteland shall
    be glad for them,
And the desert shall rejoice and blossom
    as the rose;
It shall blossom abundantly and rejoice,
Even with joy and singing.

ISAIAH 35:1–2

Don't even pretend that you haven't stood waiting for your baggage at an airport and contemplated leaping on the carousel to ride wherever it takes you in Luggage Land. Of course, being ridiculous, I did it.

We were in Africa. When we arrived at the airport, I grew bored waiting for our luggage, so I told my caregiver, Kyle, that I wanted to ride the carousel.

He looked at me like he was thinking, *Dude, have you gone mad as a cut snake?*

But Kyle came through. He hoisted me up and plopped me next to a big Samsonite suitcase. Off I went with the rest of the bags and cases. I rode the carousel through the terminal, making like a statue wearing sunglasses and drawing shocked stares, pointed fingers, and nervous laughter from the other travelers. They weren't sure if I was (a) a real person or (b) the world's most handsome duffle bag.

Finally I rode the carousel up to the little door leading to the backroom loading area. There, I was greeted by some African baggage handlers, laughing and smiling at the crazy Aussie on a joy ride.

"God bless you!" they said, cheering me on.

The baggage workers understood that sometimes even grownups have to hitch a ride on a carousel. Youth isn't wasted on children. They enjoy every minute of it. You and I should do whatever we can to keep our youthful joy alive. If your life is too predictable, don't go postal. Take a ridiculous ride back to whatever it was that gave you joy as a child. Jump on a trampoline. Saddle up a pony. Give adulthood a rest.

It's important to occasionally have a dose of ridiculous fun. It's about enjoying the ride, embracing the blessings, and always pushing not just to live but to enjoy your life to the fullest.

In my speeches, I often stand poised at the edge of my speaking platform, teetering as if I'm about to take a tumble. I tell my audiences that living on the edge isn't such a bad way to go when you have faith in yourself and in your Creator. That's not just talk. I push myself in every aspect of my life, both work and play. The most ridiculously good feeling comes over me when work and play merge into one. I encourage you to go for that feeling too.

LIMITLESS *Life*

> Live in vigorous pursuit of all the wonders that God has given us on this earth. Every now and then, cut loose and do something just for fun— something unpredictable.

16 Change Your Future

Because he has set his love upon Me,
     therefore I will deliver him;
I will set him on high, because he has
     known My name.
He shall call upon Me, and I will
     answer him;
I will be with him in trouble;
I will deliver him and honor him.
With long life I will satisfy him,
And show him My salvation.

PSALM 91:14–16

The first time I really witnessed the power of believing in one's destiny was during a high school assembly, when I heard my first motivational speaker. He was an American named Reggie Dabbs, and he had a tough job that day. There were fourteen hundred kids in our school assembly. The air was hot and sticky. The cranky sound system crackled and popped and sometimes quit.

The natives were restless, but Reggie totally captivated us with his story, telling us that he'd been born to an unmarried teenage Louisiana prostitute who had considered abortion to solve her "little problem." Fortunately for Reggie, she decided to give birth to him. She had no family and no place to live after she became pregnant, so she moved into a chicken coop.

Huddled there one night, scared and alone, she remembered that a former teacher, a very sympathetic woman, had told her to call if she ever needed help. That teacher's name was Mrs. Dabbs, and she drove from her home in Tennessee to Louisiana, picked up the pregnant teen, and took her home to her own family: a husband and six grown children. Mrs. Dabbs and her husband adopted Reggie and gave him their name.

The couple instilled in him strong moral values, Reggie said. One of the primary lessons they taught him was that no matter what his situation or circumstances, he always had the choice of responding in either a negative way or a positive way.

Reggie told us that he had almost always made the right decisions because he had faith in the possibilities for his life. He didn't want to do bad because he believed there was so much good awaiting him. He especially emphasized something that really hit home with me: "You can never change your past, but you can change your future!"

I took his words to heart. He touched all of us. Reggie also helped plant a seed in my mind about having a career as a public speaker. I liked the fact that this humble guy had a positive impact on such a big, fidgety group of teenagers in just a few minutes. It was also pretty cool that he jetted around the planet just to talk to people—he got paid to give people hope!

When I left school that day, I thought, *Maybe I'll have a good story like Reggie's to share someday.*

LIMITLESS *Life* _____

> I encourage you to accept that you may not be
> able to see a path right now, but that doesn't
> mean it's not there. Have faith; your story is still
> waiting to unfold. I know it will be incredible!

17 Blessings in Disguise

Know that the LORD, He is God;
It is He who has made us, and not we
    ourselves;
We are His people and the sheep of His
    pasture.

Enter into His gates with thanksgiving,
And into His courts with praise.
Be thankful to Him, and bless His name.
For the LORD is good;
His mercy is everlasting,
And His truth endures to all generations.

PSALM 100:3–5

After I switched my focus from my physical challenges to the blessings they presented, my life changed dramatically for the better. You can do the same. If I can recognize that the body

God gave me is in many ways a great and wondrous gift, can you acknowledge that your own blessings may also be in disguise, perhaps even dwelling within an aspect of yourself that you see as your greatest weakness?

It's all about perspective. There is no hiding from life. You will take some hits. Unless you are blasted so hard you go into a coma, you will become frustrated, angry, and sad. Been there, done that. Still, I urge you to reject despair and bitterness. You can be buried by a giant wave, or you can ride it into shore. In the same way, challenging events in your life can push you down or lift you up. If you can breathe, be grateful. Use that gratitude to rise above depression and bitterness. Take one step, then another. Build momentum and create a life you love.

My physical handicap forced me to be bold, to speak to adults and other kids, and to interact. Because of it, I focused on my strengths in mathematics so I always had a fallback profession if my speaking didn't work out. I've often thought that even some of the heartbreak I've endured because of my disability has benefited me by making me more compassionate toward others. In the same way, the failures I've experienced have made me much more appreciative of my successes and much more sympathetic to others who struggle and fail.

LIMITLESS *Life*

It isn't always easy to rise above what has
happened to you and pursue your dreams. It
takes great determination, not to mention a
sense of purpose, hope, faith, and the belief that
you have many talents and skills to share.
However, if you choose the right attitude and
gain proper perspective, you can rise above
whatever challenge you face!

_18_ Ripping the Labels Off

For this cause everyone who is godly
shall pray to You
In a time when You may be found;
Surely in a flood of great waters
They shall not come near him.
You are my hiding place;
You shall preserve me from trouble;
You shall surround me with songs of
deliverance.

PSALM 32:6–7

Remaining positive and motivated when your burden feels unbearable is difficult. We all want to fit in, but at times we all feel like outsiders.

My insecurities and doubts sprang mostly from the physical

challenges of having no arms or legs. I cannot know what your concerns are, but hanging on to hope helped me. Here is just one early experience of how it worked in my world.

I was just a toddler when my medical team recommended that my parents put me in a playgroup with other kids labeled as disabled. My parents had great love and empathy for other special-needs kids and their families, but they didn't think any child should be limited to one group of playmates. They held on to the conviction that my life would have no limits, and they fought to keep that dream alive.

My mother, bless her, made an important decision at an early stage of my life. "Nicholas, you need to play with normal children, because you are normal. You just have a few bits and pieces missing, that's all," she said, setting the tone for years to come. She didn't want me to feel less than normal or restricted in any way. She didn't want me to become introverted, shy, or insecure just because I was different physically.

Little did I realize that my parents were even then instilling in me the belief that I had every right to a life free of labels and restrictions. You have that right too. You should demand to be free of whatever categorizations or limits others try to put on you. Because of my missing bits and pieces, I am sensitive to the fact that some people accept what others say about them and unconsciously restrict themselves. Labels can provide a tempting hiding place. Some people use them as excuses.

Others rise above them. Many, many people have been labeled as handicapped or disabled only to soar above, enjoy dynamic lives, and do important things. I encourage you to rise above any attempt to restrict you from exploring and developing your gifts.

LIMITLESS *Life* _____

As a child of God, I know that He is always with me, and I'm comforted to know that He understands how much we can bear. Remember that God's arm is never too short. He can reach anyone. Draw strength from that. Dare to give it a go and to soar as high as your imagination will take you. You can expect challenges. Welcome them as character-building experiences. Learn from them and rise above them.

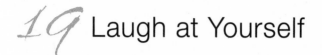 Laugh at Yourself

Have compassion on Your servants.
Oh, satisfy us early with Your mercy,
That we may rejoice and be glad all our days!
Make us glad according to the days in which
      You have afflicted us,
The years in which we have seen evil.
Let Your work appear to Your servants,
And Your glory to their children.
And let the beauty of the LORD our God
      be upon us,
And establish the work of our hands for us;
Yes, establish the work of our hands.

PSALM 90:13–17

One morning when I was thirteen, I woke up with an ugly pimple on my nose. It was a huge, ripe tomato of a pimple.

"Look at this. It's crazy," I told my mum.

"Don't scratch it," my mum said.

What would I scratch it with? I wondered.

I went to school feeling like the ugliest dude on the planet. Every time I passed a classroom and saw my reflection in the window, I wanted to run and hide. Other kids stared at it. I kept hoping it would go away, but two days later it was even bigger, the largest and reddest pimple in the universe.

The monstrous deformity would not go away! My humongous zit was still there eight months later. I felt like Rudolph the Red-Nosed Australian. Finally my mum took me to a dermatologist. I told him I wanted it removed, even if it took major surgery. He examined it with a huge magnifying glass— as if he couldn't see it—and said, "Hmm. It's not a pimple. It's a swollen oil gland." He added, "I can cut it off or burn it off, but either way, it will leave you with a scar bigger than this little red dot."

Little red dot?

"It's so big I can't see around it," I protested.

"Would you rather be scarred for life?" he asked.

The giant not-a-zit remained on my nose. I prayed and fretted about it for a while, but finally I realized that it was no more of a distraction than my lack of limbs. *If people aren't willing to talk to me, that is their loss,* I decided. If I caught someone staring at it, I made a joke. When people saw that I could laugh at myself, they laughed with me and empathized.

After all, who hasn't had a pimple? Even Brad Pitt had pimples.

Sometimes, through our own doing, we make little problems big by taking them way too seriously. Having a pimple is part of the deal. We are all perfectly imperfect human beings—some maybe more than others—but we all have our flaws and shortcomings. It's important to not take every little wart and wrinkle too seriously, because one day something truly serious will go wrong. Then what will you do?

LIMITLESS *Life*

Stand prepared to laugh at life's little knocks on the head and bumps on the nose. Laughter has been shown to reduce stress by releasing endorphin hormones, the body's natural relaxant, thereby boosting your immune system and improving your blood flow, while also increasing oxygen to the brain. Not bad, eh? Studies have also shown that laughter makes you more attractive. A double bonus!

20 Hang in There

> Be strong and of good courage, do not fear
> nor be afraid of them; for the LORD your
> God, He is the One who goes with you. He
> will not leave you nor forsake you.
>
> DEUTERONOMY 31:6

When I tell my audiences to hold on for better days, I speak from experience. You can believe and trust in what I say, because I have been there. At one point in my life I gave up hope. This low point in my mostly happy childhood came when I was around ten years old. Negative thoughts overwhelmed me. No matter how optimistic and determined and inventive I tried to be, there were some tasks I just could not do. Some of them were simple everyday activities. It really bothered me, for example, that I couldn't grab a soda out of the refrigerator like every other kid. I couldn't feed myself, and I hated to ask other people to feed me. I felt bad that they had to interrupt their meals to help me.

Other, bigger issues haunted me during this period of my life. Would I ever find a wife to love me? How would I provide for her and our children? How could I protect them if they were threatened?

I thought I'd figured out God's purpose in creating me, which was to be His partner in a miracle so the world would recognize that He was real. If He gave me arms and legs, I could go on national television, and then everyone would see the power of God.

I prayed, asking God why He couldn't give me what He'd given everyone else. *Did I do something wrong? Is that why You don't answer my prayers for arms and legs? Why won't You help me? Why do You make me suffer?*

I let my worries and fears overtake me. Everything that was wrong with me overshadowed everything that was right. I lost hope. Believe me, the loss of hope is far worse than the loss of limbs. If you have ever experienced grief or depression, you know just how bad despair can be. More than ever, I felt angry, hurt, and confused.

Most people have such thoughts. You probably have wondered at some point whether you would ever have a lasting relationship, a secure job, or a safe place to live. It is normal and healthy to look ahead, because that is how we develop a vision for our lives. The problem comes when negative thoughts block our vision for the future and cloud our minds. I pray and remind myself of the Word of God. Through it, He helps me know that He is with me. He never leaves me. He hasn't forgotten me.

LIMITLESS *Life*

> God will cause even the worst things to come together for good. Hold on to the promises of God, no matter what you see on the outside. God is good. If He allows something bad to happen, you may not understand it, but you can hold on to His goodness.

21 Now I See

Now as Jesus passed by, He saw a man who
was blind from birth. And His disciples
asked Him, saying, "Rabbi, who sinned, this
man or his parents, that he was born blind?"

Jesus answered, "Neither this man nor
his parents sinned, but that the works of
God should be revealed in him."

JOHN 9:1–3

During childhood I never dreamed there were other people in
worse circumstances than mine. Then, around age thirteen,
I read an article about a man who had been involved in a terrible accident. He was paralyzed, unable to move or talk, and
confined to a bed for the rest of his life. I couldn't imagine how
horrible that would be.

His story helped to open my eyes and expand my vision.
I realized that while my lack of limbs posed many challenges,

I still had so much to be thankful for, so many possibilities in my life.

There is great power in believing in your destiny. My awakening to the fullness of possibilities was a gradual process. At age fifteen I heard the story of the blind man in the gospel of John. He'd been blind since birth. When the disciples saw him, they asked Jesus if it was the man or his parents who had sinned that had caused him to be born blind.

It was the same question I had asked myself. *Did my parents do something wrong? Did I do something wrong? Why else would I have been born without arms and legs?*

Jesus replied, "Neither this man nor his parents sinned." Rather, he was born blind "that the works of God should be revealed in him."

When the blind man heard that explanation, it changed dramatically his vision of his life and the possibilities for it. You can imagine how this parable resonated with me as a teenager, so aware of being different, disabled, and dependent on others. Suddenly I saw that I was not a burden. I was not deficient. I was not being punished. I was custom-made for God's work to be made manifest in me, even if it didn't mean He was going to give me arms and legs!

When I read that Bible verse, a wave of peace swept over me. I'd been questioning why I was born without limbs, but now I realized that the answer was unknowable to anyone but

God, just as no one knew why that blind man was born with his disability.

Those words gave me a sense of joy and strength. For the first time I realized that the fact that I had no limbs didn't mean my Creator had abandoned me. The blind man was healed to serve His purpose. I wasn't healed, but my purpose would be revealed in time. As a boy, I had no way of knowing that my lack of limbs would help me offer my message of hope in so many nations and to so many diverse people.

Sometimes in life you won't get the answers you seek right away. You have to walk by faith. I had to learn to trust in the possibilities for my life. If I can have that trust, you can too.

LIMITLESS *Life*

> The hard times and the discouragements are not fun. You don't have to pretend to enjoy them. But believe in the possibilities for better days ahead, for a fulfilling and purposeful life.

22 Turn Off Dark Thoughts

> Put on the whole armor of God, that you
> may be able to stand against the wiles of the
> devil. For we do not wrestle against flesh and
> blood, but against principalities, against
> powers, against the rulers of the darkness of
> this age, against spiritual hosts of wickedness
> in the heavenly places.
>
> EPHESIANS 6:11–12

When I turned eleven, I entered the tricky adolescent stage when our brains rewire and strange chemicals flow throughout our bodies. Other boys and girls my age were starting to pair up, which added to my growing sense of alienation. *Would any girl ever want a boyfriend who couldn't hold her hand or dance with her?* Without even being aware of it, I allowed those dark thoughts and negative feelings to burden my spirit with growing frequency. Often they came creeping into my mind late at night when I couldn't sleep, or when I was tired after a long day at school. You know the feeling. You are so weary and out of sorts that the whole world seems to be weighing on your shoulders. We all experience downtimes, especially when lack of sleep, illness, and other challenges make us vulnerable.

No one is happy and perky 100 percent of the time. Your more somber moods are natural. They serve a purpose too. According to recent psychological studies, a darker mood can make you look at your work more critically and analytically. That outlook is helpful when you are involved in tasks like balancing your checkbook, figuring out your taxes, or editing a paper. As long as you are aware and in control of your emotions, negative thoughts can produce positive consequences. Only when you let your emotions control your actions do you risk spiraling down into depression and self-destructive behaviors.

The key is to refuse to be overwhelmed or swept away by negative emotions or feelings of depression. Fortunately, you have that power to adjust your attitude. When you detect negative thoughts running through your mind, you can choose to hit the Off switch. Acknowledge them and understand their source, but stay focused on the solutions instead of the problems. I remember from Bible class a picture of the whole armor of God, with the breastplate of righteousness, the belt of truth, the shield of faith, the sword of the Spirit, and the helmet of salvation. I'd learned that those were all the weapons a Christian boy would ever need. I see the Word of God as a sword to fight negative thoughts. You can also hold up the shield of faith to defend yourself.

LIMITLESS *Life*

> If you feel overcome by dark moods, you don't have to handle it yourself. Those who love you won't feel burdened. They want to help you. If you feel you can't confide in them, reach out to professional counselors at school, work, or in your community. You are not alone.

23 Just the Way You Are

Whatever I tell you in the dark, speak in the light; and what you hear in the ear, preach on the housetops. And do not fear those who kill the body but cannot kill the soul. But rather fear Him who is able to destroy both soul and body in hell. Are not two sparrows sold for a copper coin? And not one of them falls to the ground apart from your Father's will. But the very hairs of your head are all numbered. Do not fear therefore; you are of more value than many sparrows.

MATTHEW 10:27–31

I really am just a weird-looking bloke, I thought while staring into the mirror for several minutes after one particularly bad day. I allowed myself to wallow in grief and self-pity for a good five minutes. But then a voice from deep inside said, *Okay, like your mum says, you're missing some bits and pieces, but you have some good features too.*

I thought, *Name one. I dare you. Just find one thing. That will be enough.*

I studied my reflection a little longer and finally came up with something positive. *Girls have told me I have nice eyes. I have that, if nothing else! And no one can change that about me. My eyes will never change, so I will always have beautiful eyes.*

When you feel your spirits tumbling because you've been hurt or bullied or disparaged, go to a mirror and find one feature you love about yourself. It doesn't have to be a physical characteristic. It can be a talent, a trait, or something else. Dwell on that special something for a while. Be grateful for it, and know that your beauty and value come from the unique person you were made to be.

Don't cop out and claim, *There is nothing special about me.* We are so hard on ourselves, especially when we compare ourselves unfavorably to others. I see this especially when I talk to groups of teenagers.

That is why I make it a point to tell them, "I love you just as you are. You are beautiful to me."

The reaction to those simple words typically begins with a muffled whimper or a smothered sniffle. I'll look out to see a girl with her head down or a boy with his hands over his face. Then the powerful emotions sweep through the room like a contagion. Tears flow down young cheeks. Shoulders shake from stifled sobs. Girls huddle together. Boys leave the room to hide their faces.

After my speeches, they line up to hug me and share their feelings. Often they line up for hours.

Now, I'm a handsome enough bloke, but people don't stand in lines for hours to hug me because I'm so dashing. What really seems to be drawing them in is that I unleash a pair of powerful forces that so many are lacking in their lives: *unconditional love* and *self-acceptance.*

LIMITLESS *Life*
_____

> When you are hurt, you build walls to keep from
> being hurt again, but you can't build an interior
> wall around your heart. If you will only love
> yourself as you are, for all your natural beauty
> inside and out, others will be drawn to you, and
> they will see your beauty too.

 Outside of Yourself

As iron sharpens iron,
So a man sharpens the countenance
of his friend.

PROVERBS 27:17

When I was sixteen, I had to wait an hour after school for my ride home. Most days I'd hang out, talking to other kids or to Mr. Arnold. He wasn't the principal or even a teacher. He was the school janitor. But Mr. Arnold was one of those people who glowed from within—so at peace with himself, so comfortable in his coveralls that everyone respected him and enjoyed being around him.

Mr. Arnold was spiritual and wise and often led a Christian youth discussion at lunchtime. He invited me to join, even though I told him I wasn't big into religion. But I liked him, and so I began attending.

Mr. Arnold encouraged kids to talk openly about their lives

at these meetings, but I always turned down his invitations. For three months I refused, saying, "I don't have a story to tell."

Finally Mr. Arnold wore me down, and I consented to talk at the next meeting. I was so nervous, I prepared note cards. (Nerdy, I know.)

I wasn't expecting to impress anyone. I just wanted to get through it and get out, or so I told myself. A part of me also wanted to show the other kids that I had the same feelings, hurts, and fears that they had expressed.

For ten minutes I talked about growing up without arms and legs. I told sad stories and funny stories. Not wanting to seem like a victim, I talked about my victories. I also admitted that there were times I felt God had forgotten me, or that I'd been a mistake. I explained how I'd gradually come to understand that maybe there was a plan for me that I just hadn't figured out yet.

I was so relieved to get through my talk that I felt like crying. To my amazement, most of the kids in the room were crying instead.

"Was I that bad?" I asked Mr. Arnold.

"No, Nick," he said. "You were that good."

At first I thought he was just being nice and the kids were pretending to be moved. They were Christians, after all. They were supposed to be nice. Then one of the guys invited me to speak to his youth group. Another invitation came from a kid for his Sunday school class. Over the next two years, I received dozens of invitations to share my story with church groups, youth organizations, and service clubs.

I had avoided Christian groups in high school because I didn't want to be labeled as the religious, do-gooder preacher's kid. I acted tough and sometimes cursed so I could be accepted as a regular guy. The truth was that I had not yet accepted myself.

Obviously, God has a sense of humor. He wrangled me into speaking to just the group I had avoided, and it was there that He revealed my purpose in life. He showed me that even if I was not perfect, I had riches to share and blessings to lighten the burdens of others.

The same holds true for you. We share our imperfections. We need to share the beautiful gifts we've been given. Look inside. There is a light inside you just waiting to shine.

LIMITLESS *Life*

> My best advice for finding inner happiness is to reach outside yourself, to use your talents and brains and personality to make life better for someone else. I've been on the receiving end of that, and I'm not exaggerating when I tell you that it changed my life.

23 Celebrate Your You-niqueness

For You formed my inward parts;
You covered me in my mother's womb.
I will praise You, for I am fearfully and
      wonderfully made;
Marvelous are Your works,
And that my soul knows very well.
My frame was not hidden from You,
When I was made in secret,
And skillfully wrought in the lowest parts
      of the earth.

PSALM 139:13–15

We humans are a silly bunch. We spend half our time trying to fit in with the crowd and the other half trying to stand out from it. Why is that? It seems to be universal, part of our human nature. Why can't we be comfortable with ourselves, knowing that we are God's creations and made to reflect His glory?

As a schoolboy, I was desperate to fit in, just as most teens are. Have you ever noticed that even the teens who want to be different usually hang out with kids who dress, talk, and act just like them? What's with that, mate? How can you be an outsider if everyone you hang with wears the same black clothing, black nail polish, black lipstick, and black eyeliner? Doesn't that make you an insider instead?

Tattoos and piercings used to be a rebellious statement of rugged individualism. Now, soccer moms in the grocery have tattoos and piercings. There has to be a better way to celebrate your individuality than to follow the same fads and trends as every mum at the mall.

I've adopted an attitude that might work for you. I've decided that my beauty lies in my differences, in the fact that I'm not like everybody else. I'm uniquely me. Nobody will ever call me average or "just another guy." I may not stand tall in a crowd, but I definitely stand out.

That attitude has served me well, because I often draw strange reactions from children as well as adults when they see me for the first time. When I'm feeling frisky, I've been known to take advantage of my uniqueness. I love to cruise shopping malls with my cousins and friends. One day, a few years ago, we were in a mall when we spotted a window display for Bonds underwear, which is the down-under version of Hanes or Jockey, a brand that has been around for a long, long time.

The male mannequin was wearing a pair of Bonds "tighty whitey" underwear. He had a body just like mine: all head and torso and no limbs, but a nice six-pack of abs. I happened to be wearing my own Bond-brand drawers, so my cousins and I decided that I could serve as a window model. They hoisted me into the display case, and I took up a position next to the mannequin. Whenever window shoppers glanced at me, I twitched, smiled, winked, or bowed, to their utter shock and horror! Of course, this bit of punking provoked uproarious laughter from my co-conspirators, who were watching from outside the store. Afterward they made the case that if my public speaking career ever faltered, I could always find work as a department store dummy.

LIMITLESS *Life*

Even if you haven't always appreciated the ways you are different, thank God for His divine creation of you. Ask Him to show you how your uniqueness can be used to help others or to glorify Him.

26 Learning from Failure

I cried out to You, O Lord:
I said, "You are my refuge,
My portion in the land of the living.
Attend to my cry,
For I am brought very low;
Deliver me from my persecutors,
For they are stronger than I.
Bring my soul out of prison,
That I may praise Your name;
The righteous shall surround me,
For You shall deal bountifully with me."

PSALM 142:5–7

We can choose to respond to loss or failure by despairing and giving up, or we can let the loss or failure serve as a learning experience and motivation to do better. A friend of mine is a fitness instructor, and I've heard him tell clients who are bench-pressing weights to "go to failure." Now that's encouraging, isn't it? But the theory is that you keep pumping the iron until your muscles are exhausted. The next time, you try to exceed that limit and build more strength.

One of the keys to success in any sport and in your work, too, is practice. I think of practice as failing toward success, and I can give you a perfect example that involves me and my cell phone. You may think the smartphone is a great invention, but for me it is a gift from heaven: a single device that a guy without arms or legs can use to talk on the telephone, send e-mails and text messages, play music, record sermons and memos, and keep up with the weather and world events just by tapping it with my toes.

The smartphone isn't quite perfectly designed for me since the only part of me that can use the touch screen is a long way from the part of me that can talk! I had to figure out a way to position my cell phone closer to my mouth once I had dialed it with my foot. The method I devised gives new meaning to the term *flip phone* and offers a bruising lesson in the role of failure in success. I spent a week trying to use my little foot to flip my phone onto my shoulder, where I'd pin it down with my chin so I could talk. During this trial-and-error period, you can believe I failed many times. My face had so many bruises from being hit by the phone that I looked like I'd been smacked with a bag of nickels.

I won't tell you how many times I whacked myself in the head or nose with my cell phone or how many cell phones died in my mastering the task. I could afford to take a few hits and to replace a few cell phones. What I couldn't afford to do was give up.

Every time the cell phone cracked me in the face, I became more and more motivated to master the feat, and eventually I did! Of course, as fate would have it, shortly after I mastered the skill, the tech world came out with Bluetooth headsets that rest in your ear. Now my famous cell-phone flip is a relic of technology past. I do it occasionally to entertain friends when they're bored.

LIMITLESS *Life* ———————————————————

> Accept that there's no shame in falling short, striking out, tripping up, or screwing up. It's only a shame if you don't use the motivation from your misses and miscues to try harder and stay in the game.

27 Don't Go It Alone

Two are better than one,
> because they have a good return
> > for their work:

If one falls down,
> his friend can help him up.

But pity the man who falls
> and has no one to help him up!

Also, if two lie down together, they will keep
> > warm.

> But how can one keep warm alone?

Though one may be overpowered,
> two can defend themselves.

A cord of three strands is not quickly broken.

ECCLESIASTES 4:9–12, NIV

A strong sense of purpose, high hopes, abiding faith, self-love,
a positive attitude, fearlessness, resilience, and mastery of change

will take you a long way, but no one makes it alone. To be sure, I value my ability to take care of myself. I worked hard to become as independent as possible. But I am still dependent on the people around me, just as we all are to a great degree.

Often I am asked, "Isn't it hard to rely so much on others?" My response is, "You tell me." Whether you acknowledge it or not, you depend on those around you nearly as much as I do. Some tasks I need help managing, but no one on this earth succeeds without benefiting from the wisdom, kindness, or helping hands of someone else.

Jesus, the Son of God, rarely walked alone on this earth. He was usually in the company of one or more of His disciples. You should never feel that you have to go it alone. Asking for help is not a sign of weakness; it is a sign of strength. We all need caregivers of some sort, someone to share ideas with, someone who will always give us honest advice, or someone who serves to encourage us.

You have to be humble to ask others for help, whether it's a caregiver, a mentor, a role model, or a family member. When someone is humble enough to reach out for assistance, most people respond by giving of themselves and their time. If you act as though you have all the answers and don't need anyone else, you are less likely to attract support.

We all need supportive relationships. We all must engage with kindred spirits. To do that effectively, we must build trust and prove ourselves trustworthy. We must understand that most people instinctively act out of self-interest, but if you show them that you are interested in them and invested in their success, most will do the same for you.

LIMITLESS *Life*

> The quality of your relationships has a huge impact on the quality of your life, so treat them as precious. Don't take them for granted.

28 Another Day, Another Opportunity

Let love be without hypocrisy. Abhor what is evil. Cling to what is good. Be kindly affectionate to one another with brotherly love, in honor giving preference to one another; not lagging in diligence, fervent in spirit, serving the Lord; rejoicing in hope, patient in tribulation, continuing steadfastly in prayer; distributing to the needs of the saints, given to hospitality.

ROMANS 12:9–13

To pursue your dreams you have to take action. Move it or lose it. Act or be acted upon. If you don't have what you want, consider creating what you want. God will light the path. Your chance of a lifetime, the door to your dreams, is open. Your path to a purpose may present itself at any moment.

Even after you've built a powerful purpose and have developed huge reservoirs of hope, faith, self-esteem, positive attitudes, courage, resilience, adaptability, and good relationships, you can't just sit around and wait for a break. You have to seize upon every thread and weave a rope you can climb. Sometimes you'll even find that the boulder that fell and blocked your path also left an opening that takes you to a higher place. But you have to have the courage and determination to make the ascent.

One of our mottos at Life Without Limbs is "Another day, another opportunity." We don't simply have our slogan framed on a wall; we try to live it every day. Dr. Cara Barker, a psychologist and leadership coach, picked up on this when she wrote in a *Huffington Post* blog: "Nick Vujicic demonstrates that it's possible to awaken the heart, giving inspiration to others through a situation that nearly everyone on this Earth would find debilitating. A hero, Vujicic finds opportunity where most would find a dead end."

I'm humbled by her words. Growing up, it was often difficult for me to ever imagine myself being called a hero or an inspiration to anyone. I realized as a child that being angry about what I didn't have or frustrated about what I couldn't do only pushed people away from me, but when I looked for opportunities to serve others, people were drawn to me. I've learned not to wait around but to push ahead and make my own breaks, because one always seems to lead to another. Every time I give a speech, attend an event, or visit a new part of the world, I meet people, learn about new organizations, and gather information that opens new opportunities down the road.

LIMITLESS  _____

Develop high standards and strict criteria for evaluating how you invest your time and energy. Base your choices not on what feels good in the moment but on what best serves your ultimate goals. You will reap the rewards or pay the price for your own decisions, so choose wisely.

29 Look, Then Leap!

> Do not be deceived, God is not mocked; for
> whatever a man sows, that he will also reap.
> For he who sows to his flesh will of the flesh
> reap corruption, but he who sows to the
> Spirit will of the Spirit reap everlasting life.
> And let us not grow weary while doing good,
> for in due season we shall reap if we do not
> lose heart. Therefore, as we have opportu-
> nity, let us do good to all, especially to those
> who are of the household of faith.
>
> GALATIANS 6:7–10

One of the biggest mistakes I made early in my public speaking career was accepting an invitation to address a large audience before I'd really prepared for such a thing. It wasn't that I
had nothing to say; I just hadn't organized my material or

honed my presentation. As a result, I lacked the self-confidence to pull it off.

I stuttered and stammered through that speech. People were kind to me, but I had blown it. I learned from the experience, recovered, and realized that I should seize only those moments I am fully prepared to handle. That's not to say you shouldn't jump at an offer or an option that forces you to stretch and grow. Sometimes we're more prepared than we realize, so God gives us a nudge that allows us to rise to the occasion and take a giant step toward our dreams.

You need to weigh your options and carefully consider which steppingstones will lead you to your goals and which might cause you to slip and fall. You will come across opportunities that will serve short-term goals but not match up to your long-term objectives. Your decisions today will follow you into tomorrow.

Often, people jump into relationships without considering whether the other person is good for them over the long term. Just as you have to think carefully about how the things you post online without thinking can come back to haunt you, remember that the same is true in our lives when we evaluate the opportunities that come our way. They all have long-term consequences that can help you or hurt you. The short-term benefits may look great, but what will the long-term repercussions be?

LIMITLESS *Life*

Step back and look at the big picture. Remember, you are often tested, but life itself is not a test. It's the real deal. The decisions you make every day impact the quality of your entire life. Assess carefully, and then check your gut and your heart. If your gut tells you something's a bad idea, go with your gut. But if your heart tells you to leap at an opportunity—and it is aligned with your values and long-term goals—make the leap! There are still times when an offer gives me goose bumps, and I'm so excited I want to dive right in. But then I need to take a breath and pray for the wisdom to make the right decision.

30 Make Your Break

How much better to get wisdom than gold!
And to get understanding is to be chosen
rather than silver.

The highway of the upright is to depart
from evil;
He who keeps his way preserves his soul.

Pride goes before destruction,
And a haughty spirit before a fall.
Better to be of a humble spirit with the
lowly,
Than to divide the spoil with the proud.

He who heeds the word wisely will find good,
And whoever trusts in the LORD, happy is he.

The wise in heart will be called prudent,
And sweetness of the lips increases learning.

> Understanding is a wellspring of life to him
> who has it.
> But the correction of fools is folly.
>
> PROVERBS 16:16–22

If you have prepared yourself to the best of your ability and no doors have opened for you, then maybe you need to reposition yourself and your talents. If your dream is to be a world champion surfer, chances are you aren't going to find many big waves if you're living in Alaska, right? Sometimes you need to make a move to catch a break. I realized several years ago that if I wanted to develop a worldwide audience for my speaking career, I needed to move out of remote Australia to the wide-open United States, where I would have more options and exposure.

Even after coming to the United States, I had to work to create my own breaks. One of the best moves I made was to network with others who shared my passion for speaking and inspiring others. Studies have shown that most people learn about job openings through their professional networks of friends and coworkers. As with most other types of opportunities, you hear about them on the grapevine long before other sources have the news. Whether you are looking for love, a job, an investment, a place to volunteer, or a venue to share your talents, you can make your own breaks by joining professional groups, local clubs, the chamber of commerce, a church, a charitable crowd, or a service organization. The Internet is tailor-made for making helpful connections through social networking sites. The wider your circle, the greater your chances of finding an open door to your dream.

You shouldn't limit yourself to just those individuals, organizations, and websites related to your field of interest. Everybody knows somebody who knows somebody. So seek out anyone who is passionate and committed to a dream, even if theirs is entirely different from yours.

On the other hand, if you are hanging with a crowd of folks who don't share your dreams or your commitment to bettering your life, I'd advise you to find a new group of friends.

If you aren't attracting the kinds of offers and options you desire, maybe you need to find higher ground through higher education. If you can't win acceptance to a college or university, work your way up through community college or a tech school. More scholarships and financial aid programs are available than you might imagine, so don't let the cost discourage you. If you've already earned a degree, you may want to upgrade to a master's or a doctoral program or join a professional organization, an online community, or Internet forums and chat rooms for people in your field.

LIMITLESS *Life*

> If the breaks aren't coming your way, you need to get to the place where they can find you or you can find them.

31 Find a Creative Option

Some of you wandered for years
in the desert,
looking but not finding a good
place to live,
Half-starved and parched with thirst,
staggering and stumbling, on the
brink of exhaustion.
Then, in your desperate condition,
you called out to GOD.
He got you out in the nick of
time;
He put your feet on a wonderful
road
that took you straight to a good
place to live.

So thank GOD for his marvelous love,
 for his miracle mercy to the children
  he loves.
He poured great draughts of water down
  parched throats;
 the starved and hungry got plenty
  to eat.

PSALM 107:4–9, MSG

Albert Einstein said that in the middle of every difficulty lies opportunity. The recent recession has left millions of people unemployed. Countless others have lost their homes and their savings. What good can come of hard times?

Among the major brand-name companies that started up during recessions and depressions are Hewlett-Packard, Wrigley, UPS, Microsoft, Symantec, Toys "R" Us, Zippo, and Domino's Pizza. The founders of these companies were looking for new and better ways to serve customers because previous models had failed during downturns. They seized the moment to create their own vision for doing business.

Without a doubt, the recession of 2006–9 had a profound

and lingering impact that hurt many, many families and businesses. But many of the people cast out by corporations and longtime employers responded by starting their own businesses, going back to school for advanced degrees, or pursuing their passion in life, whether it was opening a bakery, starting a gardening service, forming a band, or writing a book.

Among those laid off or terminated in the recession were thousands and thousands of journalists. The downturn hit their industry especially hard because it occurred just as newspapers around the world were losing their lucrative classified ad business to online services like craigslist. It's been interesting to see how former journalists who prided themselves on their resourcefulness and creativity have responded. Several I know have launched careers in public relations, with nonprofit ventures, and in Web-based media and blogs.

One of my favorites is the former editor who left his shrinking California newspaper and became vice president of a booming crisis-management company that crafts "bankruptcy communications" for other businesses in decline. This is the "taking lemons and making lemonade" philosophy, which is all about shifting your focus from moaning about your problem to finding a creative solution. You have to be flexible, determined, and ready to turn a potentially negative situation into a positive situation.

LIMITLESS *Life*

It's a matter of reframing. I do it whenever my schedule hits a snag by reminding myself that "God does not waste His time, so He doesn't waste mine either." In other words, it all works out for the good. I truly believe that, and you should too. When you buy into that philosophy, stand back. I've seen it proven true time and time again.

32 The Hidden Gift

> I have learned to be content whatever the
> circumstances. I know what it is to be in
> need, and I know what it is to have plenty.
> I have learned the secret of being content in
> any and every situation, whether well fed or
> hungry, whether living in plenty or in want.
> I can do everything through him who gives
> me strength.
>
> PHILIPPIANS 4:11–13, NIV

A few years ago I was flying with my caregiver across the country. At one airport our flight was delayed (no surprise), and when we finally were on the plane and taxiing from the departure gate, I looked out the window and saw smoke coming from the engine.

A fire truck came roaring up. The firefighters jumped out and sprayed foam on the engine to put out the blaze. "Due to a small fire in the engine," the pilot told us, "we will be conducting an emergency evacuation of this plane."

Well, all right, I thought. Fire in the engine was not good, but being on the ground when the "small fire" broke out was a plus. When it was announced that our flight would be delayed two hours, many passengers complained loudly and bitterly. I was irritated but glad we had been spared a possible midflight emergency, or so I told myself.

Still, I struggled a bit to remain positive since we were on a tight schedule. *Remember, God doesn't waste time,* I told myself. Then came another announcement: they had lined up another plane at another gate to take us immediately to our destination. *Good news!*

We hurried to the new departure gate, boarded yet another plane, and settled in for the flight. I was relieved until I noticed the woman sitting next to me was quietly weeping.

"Is there something I can do?" I asked.

She explained that she was flying to visit her fifteen-year-old daughter, who was in danger of dying after a routine surgery had gone terribly wrong. I did my best to comfort the mother. We talked for nearly the entire flight. I even drew a smile from her after she told me she was nervous about flying.

"You can hold my hand if you like," I teased.

When we landed at our destination, the mother thanked me for comforting her. I told her I was grateful that I'd ended up seated next to her on the plane after so many delays and a gate change.

God had not wasted my time that day. He knew what He was doing. He put me next to that woman to help her with her fears and grief. The more I thought about that day, the more grateful I was for the chance to offer this woman a sympathetic ear.

LIMITLESS *Life*

> The next time something unforeseen happens to your plans, try not to view it as a disruption. Instead, look for the hidden gift—the opportunity that blesses you or someone around you. Be available to be used by God when He needs you!

 # Reach
and Stretch

> Take the thousand and give it to the one
> who risked the most. And get rid of this
> "play-it-safe" who won't go out on a limb.
> Throw him out into utter darkness.
>
> MATTHEW 25:28–30, MSG

I learned about risk mitigation while studying financial planning and economics in college. In the business world, as in life, it is generally conceded that you cannot avoid risk entirely, but you can manage or minimize it by measuring the depth of the muck before you wade in, no matter what sort of muck you are wading into.

There are two types of risk in life: the danger of trying and the danger of not trying. That is to say, there is always risk, no matter how you may try to avoid it or protect yourself. Let's say you are interested in dating someone. It's a gamble to call and ask the person out. You might be turned down. But what if you don't try? After all, this wonderful person might say yes. You might hit it off and live happily ever after. Remember that you have virtually no chance of living happily ever after unless you put yourself out there. Isn't that worth a tumble, mate?

You will lose now and then. You will fail. But the glory lies in getting up again and again until you succeed!

To live, you must be willing to reach and stretch. To live well, you must learn to control the odds by knowing the upside and downside before you make a move. You can't control everything that happens to you or around you, so focus on what you can control, assess every possibility you can assess, and then make a decision.

Sometimes your heart and your gut will tell you to take a chance even when the odds of success look bad on paper. You may fail. You may win. But I doubt you will ever look back with regret that you tried. I consider myself a business entrepreneur as well as a public speaker and evangelist. I've had several business and real-estate ventures over the years. I've read many books about entrepreneurs, and there is always a section on risk. Despite the image of entrepreneurs as risk takers, successful entrepreneurs are not good at taking risks; they are good at controlling and minimizing risks and then moving forward, even when they know some risk remains.

LIMITLESS *Life*

If you aren't willing to take some risks or dare to
be called crazy by those who doubt your genius,
then you likely will never achieve all that you
dream of achieving. For your sake and the
planet's, please dare to be playful too. Don't
forget to laugh at yourself and kick up your heels
now and then so that you enjoy the journey.
Don't forget to be a little ridiculous now and
again too!

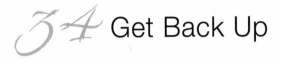 Get Back Up

Behold, all those who were incensed
                against you
Shall be ashamed and disgraced;
They shall be as nothing,
And those who strive with you shall perish.
You shall seek them and not find them—
Those who contended with you.
Those who war against you
Shall be as nothing,
As a nonexistent thing.
For I, the LORD your God, will hold your
                right hand,
Saying to you, "Fear not, I will help you."

ISAIAH 41:11–13

Sometimes, just as life appears to be flowing your way and you
are running at full steam, a serious speed bump rises up directly

in your path and *wham!* The next thing you know, friends and family are gathered around your bed, stroking your hair, patting you on the shoulder, and telling you everything will be all right.

Have you been there too? Maybe you are there now, flat on your back, feeling like the old blues song says: "Been down so long it looks like up to me."

I know the feeling all too well. In fact, in my speeches I often encourage my audiences to do whatever it takes to fight back from adversity by demonstrating my method for getting up without arms and legs. I plop down on my belly and apply my patented forehead-brace-and-crawl move to return to an upright position. I then tell the audience that even when there appears to be no way, there is always a way. I've built up a strong neck, shoulder, and chest from years of raising myself from the ground in this manner.

There are times, though, when I struggle to recover from a setback. A major crisis like a serious financial problem, a lost job, a broken relationship, or the loss of a loved one can be difficult for anyone to manage. Even a relatively minor challenge can seem overwhelming if you are already wounded or vulnerable. If you find yourself struggling more than usual with a challenge, my recommended recovery plan is to lean with gratitude on those who care about you, be patient with your tender feelings, do your best to understand the realities versus the emotions at play, and put your faith into action. As hard as it may seem, move forward one step at a time, day by day, knowing that there will be valuable lessons learned and strength gained in each trial.

I suggest a three-step approach to accomplish this. First, you need to make internal adjustments to manage your emotions so they don't manage you. This will allow you to take control of your life and respond thoughtfully one step at a time. Second, remind yourself of how you have persevered through adversity in the past and emerged stronger and wiser for the experience. Third, reach out not only to seek help and encouragement from others but to give them too. There is healing power in receiving as well as in giving.

LIMITLESS *Life*

There is a certain peace to be found in knowing that there is a master plan for your life and that your value, purpose, and destiny are not determined by what happens to you but by how you respond to it.

33 Meltdown Management

Reproach has broken my heart,
And I am full of heaviness;
I looked for someone to take pity,
	but there was none;
And for comforters, but I found none.
They also gave me gall for my food,
And for my thirst they gave me vinegar
	to drink.

PSALM 69:20–21

In December 2010 I hit a wall. I had a meltdown that sent me reeling for an extended period, longer than any other time in my adult life. Although I would not wish hard times on anyone, major meltdowns are a part of life. I like to believe that rough patches are meant to teach me important things about myself, such as the strength of my character and the depth of my faith. You have probably experienced your own meltdowns, and I'm sure you've taken away lessons learned. Personal, career, or financial crises are all too common and often difficult to recover from emotionally. But if you see them as opportunities for learning and growth, you will likely bounce back stronger and more quickly.

If your despair does not ease in a reasonable amount of time, or if you feel depressed over long periods, please reach out for help either to someone you trust or to a counselor. Some forms of emotional trauma require professional help. There is no shame in taking advantage of expert care. Millions of people have been relieved of their severe depression in this way.

Paralyzing sadness, despair, and grief brought on by hard times or tragedies can strike anyone. Unexpected and stressful events can leave us feeling overwhelmed and emotionally beaten, bruised, and battered. It's important that you don't isolate yourself in these situations. Allow your family and friends to console you. Be patient with them and with yourself.

Healing takes time. Few people can simply just snap out of it, so don't expect that to happen. Know that you have to work at healing. It's not a passive process. You must flip the switch and tap into whatever power runs through you, including your willpower and the power of your faith.

I wish I could tell you that my meltdown went away as quickly as it came on, that one morning I awoke with a clear head and a renewed spirit, jumped out of bed, and announced, "I'm baaack!" Sorry, but it didn't happen that way for me, and if you go through a similar rough period, you probably won't pop right out of it either. Just know that better days are ahead, and this too shall pass.

LIMITLESS *Life* _____

> Your comeback, like mine, may come in small steps, day by day, over a period of weeks or months. I hope yours comes quickly, but there are benefits to a gradual revival. As the fog of despair lifts, be grateful for every ray of light that comes through.

36 Reality Check

Therefore I will not restrain my mouth;
I will speak in the anguish of my spirit;
I will complain in the bitterness of my soul.
Am I a sea, or a sea serpent,
That You set a guard over me?
When I say, "My bed will comfort me,
My couch will ease my complaint,"
Then You scare me with dreams
And terrify me with visions,
So that my soul chooses strangling
And death rather than my body.
I loathe my life;
I would not live forever.
Let me alone,
For my days are but a breath.

JOB 7:11–16

During my meltdown I experienced something you may have noticed in your own trials. As stress opened old wounds and insecurities, my perception of what was going on became much worse than the reality of the situation. One tip-off that your response is out of sync with the actual situation is the use of inflated and exaggerated descriptions, such as these:

"This is killing me."

"I will never recover from this!"

"This is absolutely the worst thing that's ever happened to me."

"Why does God hate me?"

And the always popular: "My life is destroyed. Forever!"

I will not admit to saying any of those things during my tribulations, but some people who were in my vicinity might have thought they heard similar lamentations. Or worse!

I am honored to provide you with a good example of a bad example from my own behavior. The wielding of such over-the-top language should have served as a warning that my despair was excessive.

These were my perceptions of what was going on: *I'm a failure! I'm going to go bankrupt! My worst fears are realized! I'm not able to support myself! I'm a burden on my parents! I'm not worthy of love!*

This was the reality of what was occurring: My business

was experiencing a temporary cash-flow problem during a period of economic recession. We were fifty thousand dollars in the red, which was not good, but it certainly was not an overwhelming deficit, given the prospects for growth in the global demand for our products and services. I majored in accounting and financial planning in college, and economics was part of that curriculum. I knew about supply and demand and cash flow, but what I knew was clouded by what I felt.

LIMITLESS *Life*

You may have experienced a similar sensation of being totally overwhelmed even though the actual situation wasn't nearly as devastating as it seemed. Our vision can be impaired by our feelings, and in the midst of despair it can be very difficult to look at things realistically.

37 Learning from Loss

When times get bad, people cry out for help.
They cry for relief from being kicked
around,
But never give God a thought when things
go well,
when God puts spontaneous songs
in their hearts,
When God sets out the entire creation as a
science classroom,
using birds and beasts to teach wisdom.

JOB 35:9–11, MSG

Once my head began to clear of the self-defeating thoughts I conjured up during my meltdown, I appreciated the time I was given to reflect and contemplate my plunge into the abyss.

I examined my actions and their impact on my life. I found I had been driving myself because I thought the success of my endeavors depended on me. In fact, I should have trusted in God and relied more on His strength and His will and His timing. I should have been putting my faith into action.

The worst times that test your faith can be the best times for renewing it and putting it into action. A wise soccer coach told me that he values losing as much as winning, because losing reveals weaknesses and failings that have probably been there all along and need to be addressed for lasting success. Losses also motivate players to work on the skills they need to master in order to win.

When life is going well, we don't often stop and assess it. Most of us examine our lives, careers, and relationships only when we aren't getting the desired results. In every setback, failure, and defeat there are valuable lessons to be learned and even blessings to be unlocked.

In the early days of my despair, I wasn't much in the mood for seeking out the lessons. Nevertheless, they found me over time, and the blessings revealed themselves too. I don't like to reflect on that period, but I still force myself to revisit it, because new layers unfold and more lessons emerge with every visit. I encourage you to look for the learning points in your own challenges. You may be tempted to put hard times behind you and out of your mind. No one likes to feel vulnerable. It's certainly no fun recalling how I wallowed in my misery, held pity parties, and grossly overreacted to what proved to be a temporary setback.

Yet one of the best ways to take the pain out of past experiences is to replace the hurt with gratitude. My cousins put their own spin on it, saying, "Dude, it's all good in the hood!"

LIMITLESS *Life*

It should go without saying that putting your faith into action is not a passive exercise. You have to actively and willfully take the necessary steps to locate and move along the path God designed for you. When you fall off the path, as I did, at some point you have to ask yourself what happened, why it happened, and what you need to do to resume your journey of faith and purpose.

38 A Perspective on Fear

Then He said to His disciples, "Therefore I say to you, do not worry about your life, what you will eat; nor about the body, what you will put on. Life is more than food, and the body is more than clothing. Consider the ravens, for they neither sow nor reap, which have neither storehouse nor barn; and God feeds them. Of how much more value are you than the birds? And which of you by worrying can add one cubit to his stature? If you then are not able to do the least, why are you anxious for the rest? Consider the lilies, how they grow: they neither toil nor spin; and yet I say to you, even Solomon in all his glory was not arrayed like one of these. If then God so clothes the grass, which today is in the field and tomorrow is thrown into the oven, how

much more will He clothe you, O you of
little faith?

LUKE 12:22–28

One of the lessons I learned is that you have to keep things in
perspective, even when you are in the middle of a personal
crisis. Fear breeds fear, and worry builds upon worry. You cannot stop the feelings of grief, remorse, guilt, anger, and fear
that wash over you during difficult times, but you can recognize them as purely emotional responses and then manage
them so they don't dictate your actions.

Maintaining perspective requires maturity, and maturity
comes with experience. I had never been through a situation
like this, and because I was physically drained by all my travels, I had a difficult time handling this financial crisis in a mature manner.

My father and other older and wiser friends and family
members tried to help me by telling me they'd been through
similar or worse experiences and had bounced back. My uncle
Batta is in the real-estate development and property manage-
ment business in California. You can imagine the ups and
downs he has seen. An operating deficit of fifty thousand

dollars is small change in his business, and he tried to tell me that it was not a crippling debt for mine either.

Still, as much as I would like to learn from other people's advice and mistakes, for the longest time I seemed to need to make my own blunders before I gained any true wisdom. I've now resolved to be a better student. If you and I can learn just one lesson from every person we know, how much wiser would we be? How much time, effort, and money would we save?

When our loved ones and friends give advice, why can't we listen, absorb the lesson, and make the necessary adjustments? You only increase your stress by thinking you have to fix things *right now*! True, some crises demand immediate action, but that action can include a step-by-step, one-day-at-a-time approach to problem solving.

LIMITLESS *Life*

A member of my advisory board asked me, "Nick, do you know the best way to eat an entire elephant? One bite at a time." Remember this the next time you need to do something that seems overwhelming!

39 A Shining Faith

You are the light of the world. A city that is
set on a hill cannot be hidden. Nor do they
light a lamp and put it under a basket, but
on a lampstand, and it gives light to all who
are in the house. Let your light so shine
before men, that they may see your good
works and glorify your Father in heaven.

MATTHEW 5:14–16

While we may not always be faithful to God, He is always
faithful to us. I had not been consciously putting my faith into
action each and every day. I resolved to do that, not just to
pray, but to move forward with perspective, patience, humility,
courage, and confidence each day, knowing that God is strong
where I am weak, and God will provide what I lack.

Faith, whether it is faith in yourself and your purpose or

faith in your Creator, is a powerful beacon, but you have to let its light shine. You cannot allow it to be dimmed by neglect. Sometimes you may feel like you have faith, but no light is showing. I realized I had to let my faith shine. From a different perspective, my faith had become like a car with the transmission in neutral. It was there, but it was not engaged. Having faith in yourself and your abilities is critical, but you must also have patience, humility, and the understanding that you cannot do anything without the help of others. Above all, in the end, all credit goes to God.

Nothing will bring you down faster than living without purpose or losing track of whatever you are most passionate about, the gift that gives you joy and makes your life meaningful. I lost track of my purpose to inspire and encourage others while spreading the message of faith. I was trying to do too many other things to build my business and charity. When I strayed from my true purpose, it was as if someone pulled the plug on my power cord.

If you feel yourself sliding into despair, drained of energy and depleted of faith, ask yourself, *What matters most to me? What gives me joy? What drives me and gives my life meaning? How can I get back to that?*

You and I were put on this earth to serve something greater than our own narrow interests. When our focus becomes self-centered instead of God-centered, we lose our greatest source of power. Our God-given talents are meant to benefit others. When we use them for that greater purpose, we put faith into action to fulfill His plan for us. We make a difference in this world that helps prepare us for the next.

LIMITLESS *Life*

God does not love you because you are successful at school or work. He does not love you because you are better at some task than someone else. God loves you because He created you. God loves you for you.

40 Hearing Your Life's Calling

Trust in the LORD, and do good;
Dwell in the land, and feed on His
      faithfulness.
Delight yourself also in the LORD,
And He shall give you the desires
      of your heart.

Commit your way to the Lord,
Trust also in Him,
And He shall bring it to pass.
He shall bring forth your righteousness
      as the light,
And your justice as the noonday.

PSALM 37:3–6

Early in my life, when my parents were trying to look ahead and figure out what sort of future I might have, my father, an accountant, suggested that I follow into his profession. "You are good with numbers, and you can always hire other people to be your arms and legs," my dad said.

Crunching numbers is fun for me. Counting on my fingers and toes is not an option, but thanks to modern technology and my little foot, I can use a calculator and computer easily enough. So in college I went along with the parental plan and majored in financial planning and accounting. The thought of helping people make good monetary decisions, creating wealth for them, and mapping out strategic plans for sustenance appealed to me. I also enjoyed trading in the stock market, where I've had both good and bad experiences.

Working as a financial planner seemed like a good way to serve others while supporting myself and, one day, my family too. Still, I never felt fully committed to that plan. There was always the sense that God was calling on me to follow a different path. I'd begun giving talks about my disabilities to my junior high classmates. They responded to my words. I touched something in them, and God lit the sparks of a passion He'd placed within me.

Over time, I spoke more and more about my faith. Evangelism and inspiration became my greatest passions. Speaking about my love of God and the blessings in my life, including my disabilities and the strength they have given me, allows me to serve others. It's given my life a purpose, one that I believe God created for me.

That is a great gift. Many people struggle to find meaning and direction in their lives. They question their value because they aren't clear on how they can contribute or make a mark. Maybe you haven't identified where your talents and interests lie. It's not uncommon to cast about trying one thing or another before identifying your life's calling. Changing course several times is increasingly common.

I encourage you to identify whatever it is that fulfills you and engages all your gifts and energy. Pursue that path, not for your own glory or enrichment, but to honor God and to make a contribution. Be patient if it takes time to find your way.

LIMITLESS *Life*

Know that timing is important. As long as you hold a true passion in your heart, it will not fade. Understand that even passions come with some risk. Remember, too, that if one passion ends, it is probably because God has something bigger and better in mind for you.

41 A Passionate Pursuit

> As long as it is day, we must do the work of
> him who sent me. Night is coming, when
> no one can work.
>
> JOHN 9:4, NIV

US Marine Victor Marx is a martial arts expert who holds a seventh-degree black belt in Keichu-Do self-defense, which incorporates elements of karate, judo, jiujitsu, boxing, American wrestling, and street fighting. He has trained more than thirty world champions in the martial arts as well as operators from Navy Seals, Army Rangers, and Delta Force.

Looking at him, you would be shocked to know that he once considered himself to be damaged goods. He told me that he and I have much in common, except that my disability challenges are very visible while his are hidden from sight, locked inside his mind and spirit.

As a child, Victor never knew his father, who had a history of dealing drugs and promoting prostitution. Victor thought his first stepfather was his real father. His mother divorced and married six times. He and his siblings were raised in dysfunction and chaos.

Victor suffered unspeakable cruelty. One stepfather tortured him, held his head underwater, and put a gun to his head. He was sexually and physically abused between the ages of three and seven. Once he was molested and left for dead in a locked commercial cooler.

So much had been inflicted on him that Victor could not manage all of the pain. He underwent counseling, and his doctors explained his posttraumatic stress disorder, which is common in victims of childhood abuse. One psychiatrist told him that his brain had been scrambled by the horrors he had endured, so his mind did not process thoughts in a normal manner and never would.

Along with the professional treatment for his PTSD, Victor's powerful faith helped him learn to deal with revived memories and the trauma they triggered. Over time, he shared the story of his childhood and his walk of faith. He found an especially receptive audience in troubled young people, including juvenile offenders, gang members, youth prison inmates, foster care kids, and residents of drug treatment centers.

"I had lived with so much denial, I didn't realize I even had a story, and I wasn't sure I should be telling it," he said, but he discovered that his story resonates with troubled young people because many of them have suffered physical and sexual abuse as children too.

To Victor's surprise, many churches requested that he speak to their congregations and share his story of redemption. His story offers testimony to the power of faith through his victory over a tragic childhood and his pursuit of a passion to serve troubled young people.

Once he began sharing his story, Victor could not keep up with the requests for speaking engagements. To his great surprise, unsolicited donations began arriving in the mail. In 2003, he and his wife formed a nonprofit evangelistic organization, All Things Possible, and two years later they received a surprise $250,000 donation from a couple who had heard of his work and wanted to support it.

"We were worried that we'd never be able to support ourselves doing this type of work, but we've seen unbelievable things happen since we committed to it and put our faith in God."

LIMITLESS *Life*

There are many ways to make a contribution while pursuing your passion. Your unique package of talents, education, and experience may be suited for business, public service, the arts, tradecrafts, evangelism, or other fields. The important thing is to recognize what God has put in you and to build your life around those gifts and passions even if you don't fully understand where it will lead you.

God Pays for What He Orders!

May the God of peace, who through the
blood of the eternal covenant brought back
from the dead our Lord Jesus, that great
Shepherd of the sheep, equip you with
everything good for doing his will, and
may he work in us what is pleasing to him,
through Jesus Christ, to whom be glory for
ever and ever. Amen.

HEBREWS 13:20–21, NIV

You'll know you've found a passion when your talents, knowledge, energy, focus, and commitment come together in a way
that excites you like a child with a favorite game or toy. Your
work and pleasure become one and the same. What you do
becomes part of who you are.

Your passion leads you to your purpose, and both are activated when you share your gifts with the world. You are custommade for your purpose, just as I am for mine. Every part of you—from your mental, physical, and spiritual strengths to your unique package of talents and experiences—is designed to fulfill that gift.

If you haven't found the work God intended for you, ask yourself these questions: What drives you? What makes you excited about each day? What would you do for free just to be doing it? What would you never want to retire from doing? Is there something you would give up everything else for—all of your material possessions and comforts—just to do because you feel so good doing it? What do you feel a sense of urgency about accomplishing?

If that doesn't help you identify a passion, try asking those closest to you for their assessments and suggestions.

Finally, before you decide what your passion may be, check in with the ultimate authority on the subject. Pursue God's love and get to know Him as a friend so you can enjoy His presence. Pray for guidance and meditate on His Word. Ask others to pray for you as well.

I assure you, God pays for what He orders. He would not call you into His service without providing all you need to pursue your passion and purpose. At first you may not understand your calling. You may think that you lack any passion for it.

My dad was called to start a church, which he had no interest in doing. Yet he honored God and did what he felt called to do. I'm sure Noah, too, had doubts when God put in an order for an enormous ark, but he didn't say a word. He just built the boat. Following that order turned out to be a wise move.

LIMITLESS *Life*

When God calls you to do something, you may not understand or be enthusiastic at first, but you should always be passionate about Him, which means you will do anything for Him.

 # Leaders Who
Serve Others

For I say, through the grace given to me, to
everyone who is among you, not to think of
himself more highly than he ought to think,
but to think soberly, as God has dealt to each
one a measure of faith. For as we have many
members in one body, but all the members
do not have the same function, so we, being
many, are one body in Christ, and individu-
ally members of one another.

ROMANS 12:3–5

You can sow good seeds, no matter where you are in life, no
matter what your circumstances might be. Whether you are
the founder of a huge charitable operation, the leader of a
nation, the pastor of a parking lot ministry that serves the

homeless, or a volunteer at your church, the godly work that you do as a servant leader is magnified many times over because of all the lives you touch.

All of the servant leaders I've met in my travels share certain characteristics and attitudes that we should all adopt and emulate. First of all, they are incredibly humble and selfless. Many of them give their entire lives to the service of others, and they do not care at all if they receive recognition. Instead of standing at the forefront, most would rather be at the back of the room urging on their volunteers and encouraging those they serve. They would rather give credit than receive it.

Servant leaders also are great listeners and empathizers. They listen to understand the needs of those they serve, and they also observe and empathize to pick up on unexpressed needs. Usually people don't have to come to them to ask for help, because they've already picked up on what is needed. Servant leaders operate with this thought in mind: *If I were in this person's situation, what would comfort me? What would build me up? What would help me overcome my circumstances?*

They are healers, really. They provide solutions while others ponder problems. For example, I'm sure many good people looked at the suffering and illness afflicting people in third world countries and saw this immense problem: how could you possibly build enough hospitals in those remote, impoverished areas to serve all those in need? Don and Deyon

Stephens saw past the problem and came up with an ingenious solution: convert cruise ships into floating hospitals and staff them with volunteers who travel to wherever there is need. Thus began the Mercy Ship Ministry.

Servant leaders also don't bother with short-term fixes. They sow seeds that will have lasting, long-term, and ever-expanding impact. Planters of good seeds keep building on what they've done, either by growing it themselves or inspiring others to join and surpass.

Finally, servant leaders are bridge builders who put aside narrow self-interests in favor of harnessing the power of many to bring change for the benefit of all. They believe in abundance, that there are rewards enough for everyone when both goals and successes are shared. Where some leaders believe in dividing and conquering, servant leaders believe in building a community of people with a common purpose.

LIMITLESS *Life* _____

> When you serve others, your own heart heals. I encourage you to sow good seeds by serving others. You may find that the life you transform is your own.

 # Helping Others

Finally, all of you be of one mind, having
compassion for one another; love as brothers,
be tenderhearted, be courteous; not returning evil for evil or reviling for reviling, but
on the contrary blessing, knowing that you
were called to this, that you may inherit a
blessing.

1 PETER 3:8–9

Leon Birdd was driving in a rural area just outside Dallas in
1995 when he saw a middle-aged man walking with great difficulty along a service road. At first, Leon had no inclination to
pick up the stranger, whom he thought might be drunk. But
he felt the Holy Spirit speak to his heart, so he turned his truck
around and drove back to offer the man a ride.

"Are you okay? I'll give you a ride," Leon said.

"I'm not drunk," the man insisted gruffly.

The man, Robert Shumake, was telling the truth. He had difficulty walking because he'd undergone several brain surgeries, which affected his mobility but not his determined efforts to help others in need. Every Saturday morning for years the gruff-talking Robert had been taking doughnuts and coffee to feed the homeless in downtown Dallas.

"How do you do that when you can hardly walk?" Leon asked.

"People help me, and now you'll help me," he said.

"I don't think so. What time do you do this?" Leon asked.

"Five thirty in the morning."

"I am not going to drive you, especially at that hour," Leon said. "Even the Lord isn't up at five thirty in the morning."

Robert would not take no for an answer. He told Leon where to pick him up. "You'll be there," he said.

"Don't count on it," Leon replied.

The next Saturday, Leon awakened at five o'clock, worried that Robert might be waiting for him on a street corner in a rough part of the city. Once again, the Holy Spirit seemed to be working through him.

Before sunrise, he found Robert standing on a street corner with a thermos filled with five gallons of hot coffee. Robert asked Leon to drive him to a doughnut shop, where they loaded up on pastries. They then proceeded to a rough patch of downtown Dallas. The streets were empty. "Just wait," Robert told Leon.

With the big thermos of steaming coffee sitting on a curb, they waited. As the sun rose in the sky, homeless men and women appeared one by one. Nearly fifty of them assembled for Robert's coffee and doughnuts.

Although Robert had a rough way of talking to the people he served, they welcomed the warm coffee and doughnuts. Leon, who had given his life to Christ a couple years earlier, saw that Robert was sowing good seeds and that he clearly needed help. So he began assisting him each Saturday morning after that.

In the months that followed, Robert's health declined.

"Robert, what happens when you can't do this anymore?" Leon asked one day as they packed up.

"You'll do it," Robert said.

"No, you really need to get someone else," Leon insisted.

"You will do it," Robert said again.

Robert was right. Leon Birdd became Pastor Birdd, an ordained minister with an inner-city mission supported by nine local churches and other donors.

Although Robert died in 2009, the seeds he planted have been nurtured and grown by Pastor Birdd and his wife, Jennifer. Today, those street-corner meetings for coffee and doughnuts are full-blown, open-air services with music and celebrations of faith. Now, every Sunday morning, more than fifty volunteers join Pastor Birdd in feeding the bodies and ministering to the souls of hundreds of homeless in a downtown Dallas parking lot.

LIMITLESS *Life*

> Every individual who knows God understands that all people need love and encouragement, even if it is just a kind word or a smile to go with a doughnut and hot coffee.

Wisdom from
a Role Model

I'm not saying that I have this all together,
that I have it made. But I am well on my way,
reaching out for Christ, who has so wondrously
reached out for me. Friends, don't get me
wrong: By no means do I count myself an
expert in all of this, but I've got my eye on the
goal, where God is beckoning us onward—
to Jesus. I'm off and running, and I'm not
turning back.

So let's keep focused on that goal, those of
us who want everything God has for us. If any
of you have something else in mind, something
less than total commitment, God will clear your
blurred vision—you'll see it yet! Now that we're
on the right track, let's stay on it.

PHILIPPIANS 3:12–16, MSG

One of my long-term role models whom I had always wanted to meet is the evangelist Billy Graham. In 2011, at the invitation of his daughter, Anne Graham Lotz, I finally had an opportunity to do just that. My wife, Kanae, and I were honored and thrilled to meet Reverend Graham at his North Carolina mountain home.

Health problems have limited his public appearances in recent years, but the ninety-two-year-old evangelist still looms large as an international figure. Anne, who was with us that day, had cautioned us that her father had been ill with pneumonia and other afflictions. She said he might tire easily, but although he appeared frail, when he spoke, his voice was strong and very familiar to someone who had so often heard him speak.

"When Anne told me you were coming, I was very excited, because I've been hearing about your ministry," he said. "The Lord woke me at three this morning to pray for our meeting."

Reverend Graham let me know that he saw me as one of the next generation, an heir to his evangelistic mission, and he wanted to prepare me with words of wisdom and encouragement. He said we were in exciting times and that no matter what adversity we had to go through, our job was to preach the gospel of Jesus Christ.

It was a wonderful meeting. Talking to him was similar to

speaking with an Old Testament figure like Abraham or Moses, because Reverend Graham has been such a key person in our spiritual lives for so long.

He touched us deeply in his humanity. He humbly reflected on his life while nibbling on chocolate chip cookies. He said his only regrets were that he had not memorized more scripture and, in a testament to his faith, Reverend Graham said that he should have spent more time at the feet of Jesus, telling Him how much he loves Him!

I'm sure Reverend Graham has forgotten more scripture than the rest of us could ever memorize, and I'm equally certain that he expressed his love for our Lord far more than most. Yet this legendary evangelist, who has also talked about wishing he'd spent more time with his family, wishes he had done even more to show his faith and love of God.

LIMITLESS *Life* _____

> Are you so caught up in the day-to-day challenges of making a living, overcoming obstacles, dealing with circumstances, or just surviving that you have neglected relationships, spiritual growth, a deeper understanding of the world, or your health?

 Living in Balance

You're blessed when you stay on course,
 walking steadily on the road revealed
 by God.
You're blessed when you follow his
 directions,
 doing your best to find him.
That's right—you don't go off on your
 own;
 you walk straight along the road he set.
You, God, prescribed the right way to live;
 now you expect us to live it.
Oh, that my steps might be steady,
 keeping to the course you set;
Then I'd never have any regrets
 in comparing my life with your
 counsel.
I thank you for speaking straight from
 your heart;
 I learn the pattern of your righteous
 ways.

I'm going to do what you tell me to do;
don't ever walk off and leave me.

PSALM 119:1–8, MSG

Listening to Reverend Graham reflect on his long and illustrious career as an evangelist causes me to step back and think about what I want to look back on when I reach a similar place in my life.

You and I should not live with the expectation that happiness will come *some* day when we accomplish *some* goal or acquire *some* thing. Happiness should be available to you in every moment, and the way to access it is to live in balance spiritually, mentally, emotionally, and physically.

One way to determine the balance that works for you is to look ahead to the end of your life and then live so that you will have no regrets when you arrive there. The idea is to create a clear image of the type of person you want to become as you age and the mark you hope to make, so that every step of your journey takes you closer to where you want to end up.

I believe if you create in your imagination the life you want to live, it is then possible to create it minute by minute, hour by hour, and day by day in reality. Some advise that the way to do this is to think about your own funeral and ponder what you would want your family and friends to say about you, your character, your accomplishments, and how you influenced their lives. Maybe that works for you, but I don't like to think about leaving my loved ones behind—even if I'm going to be with God in heaven.

Instead, I prefer to put myself in Reverend Graham's position on that day we met in his mountain cabin. Here was a great man nearing the end of a remarkable, faith-filled life in which he had done so much work for the Lord, and he still had regrets. It may be inevitable. Few achieve a perfectly balanced life, but I think it's worth a try, don't you?

LIMITLESS *Life* _____

I don't want to have any regrets at all, which may not be possible, but I'm going to do my best. So I've reset the Nick life-meter with the needle on Balance. You might take a moment to do the same if you feel, as I do, that we all need to pause now and then to examine where we've been, where we are now, where we want to go, and how to become a person who will be remembered for making a positive difference in the world.

47 "God-is-abled"

Fear not, for I am with you;
Be not dismayed, for I am your God.
I will strengthen you,
Yes, I will help you,
I will uphold you with My righteous
   right hand.

ISAIAH 41:10

When I'm asked how I can claim a ridiculously good life when I have no arms and legs, my inquisitors assume I'm suffering from what I lack. They inspect my body and wonder how I could possibly give my life to God, who allowed me to be born without limbs. Others have attempted to soothe me by saying that God has all the answers and that when I'm in heaven I will find out His intentions. Instead, I choose to believe and live by what the Bible says, which is that God is the answer today, yesterday, and always.

When people read about my life or witness me living it, they are prone to congratulate me for being victorious over my disabilities. I tell them that my victory came in surrender. It comes every day when I acknowledge that I can't do this on my own, so I say to God, "I give it to You!" Once I yielded, the Lord took my pain and turned it into something good, which brought me real joy.

What was that "something good"? For me, it was purpose and significance. My life mattered. When I could not find meaning and purpose for my life, I surrendered the need to do that, and God stepped in. He gave my life meaning when no one and nothing else could provide it.

Here's another way to understand what happens in my life each day. Put the word *Go* in front of the word *disabled,* and with a little creative visualization, you'll suddenly be looking at "God-is-abled." There you have it. I may be *disabled,* but God is *abled.* He makes all things possible. Where I am weak, He is strong. Where I have limitations, He has none. So my life without limits is the result of my surrendering to Him all of my plans, dreams, and desires. I don't quit, but I do surrender. I give up all of my plans so He can show me His path for me.

If you have surrendered in faith to God, and life keeps throwing obstacles at you, tap into His grace and say, "If it is Your will that I achieve this dream, help me." I believe God's path is the one that leads us to fulfilling our greatest potential.

My advice is to know all you can and then surrender the outcome to His knowledge. Over time the puzzle will work itself out. As the Bible says, "His wisdom is profound, his power is vast" (Job 9:4, NIV).

LIMITLESS *Life*

You may be preparing to make a move, standing on the ledge but paralyzed by fear because you aren't sure you can do it. Try giving it to Him instead. What will it take for you to trust this to God? I encourage you to count the cost of what your life might be like without Him, without the Lord in all your decisions. Believe His promises for you today. Let Him be your joy and satisfaction. Ask God to be the one to define the purpose of your life and for your life. Ask Him for the faith you'll need to do so.

 # 48 Full Surrender

> The LORD is my strength and song,
> And He has become my salvation;
> He is my God, and I will praise Him;
> My father's God, and I will exalt Him.
>
> EXODUS 15:2

You and I tend to want answers now, but we have to trust that God has His own timetable. If we stay in faith and seek understanding, His plan will be revealed when we are ready for the answer. The purpose of a child born without arms or legs was a mystery revealed slowly as I grew in faith. As I've often noted, one of the keys for me was reading in the Bible about the man born blind (John 9:1–3). Jesus performs a miracle to heal him and explains that His purpose for this man was to use him to display God's glory. This scripture helped me realize that God might also have a purpose for me. Maybe, like the man born without sight, I'd been created without arms and legs so that God could deliver a message or somehow work through me.

As my understanding of God's ways and life's opportunities increased, He patiently put me on His path and opened my eyes to my purpose.

I believe that when you surrender your life in full, with complete trust and patience, there is another great reward that comes your way: God's strength. Since the age of eighteen, I have traveled the world, often visiting twenty or more countries each year. I'm not flying in private jets. The places I travel to are often dangerous, difficult to reach, and unhealthy due to disease, poor water quality, and lack of modern medical care. Yet somehow God keeps me healthy and gives me the strength to carry His message to millions of people.

I have come to understand that surrender brings strength.

You and I may like to think we are in command of our lives, our comings and our goings, but once we commit our lives to Him, God is in command every minute of every day. Our gracious heavenly Father often overrides my carefully made plans by revealing His own deep, unfathomable ways, and I am humbled every time. I marvel at the beauty and pure brilliance of God's divine plan each time. Sometimes I imagine what it must have been like to have been a disciple and an apostle and a witness to God at work through Jesus on earth as

He moved in indescribable ways. I can almost picture His followers returning to their own congregants, who were scattered across the Roman Empire, and reporting, "You'll never believe what God did!"

LIMITLESS *Life*

The power of Jesus is here. When you put your faith in action by surrendering all to Him, you won't believe what God will do for you. I promise you will discover an exciting life when you put yourself in His hands. Look forward, then, to a life in faith, believing that Christ intends to use us as we intentionally surrender to His hope-filled, meaningful purposes for us. Allow His cleansing love to flow freely and at full force through your life. As the psalm tells us, "Taste and see that the LORD is good" (34:8).

49 Loved by God

For God so loved the world that He gave His
only begotten Son, that whoever believes in
Him should not perish but have everlasting
life. For God did not send His Son into the
world to condemn the world, but that the
world through Him might be saved.

JOHN 3:16–17

God sees the beauty and value of all His children. His love is
the reason we are here. You were created for a purpose, and
over time it will be revealed to you. Know that where you feel
weak, God will give you strength. All you have to do is reach
out to those who love you, to those who want to help you,
and most of all to your Creator by asking Him to come into
your life.

God has a plan for you. It's called salvation, and it's worth sticking around to see what He has in store for you both in this world and in heaven everlasting.

One problem I've seen with many people is that they don't trust that our God is a loving God. Somewhere they've come up with a view of God as a vengeful enforcer poised to strike down anyone who doesn't follow His commandments. If they've made mistakes or not lived a perfect life—whatever that is—they feel they will never be worthy of God's love. That is not true! Our loving Father always stands ready to forgive you and to welcome you into His arms.

The Bible does say we are supposed to fear God, which doesn't mean that you should cower in terror or hide from His wrath. Instead, it is a call for us to treat Him with respect and obedience while acknowledging His greatness. The Bible also says, "God is love" (1 John 4:8). We should never forget that He loves us so much that He sent His Son down from heaven to die on the cross. So while we should respect God, we should always remember He loves us too.

He is waiting for you to let Him heal you. He doesn't have to heal you physically; He just has to heal your heart. He will give you peace, love, and joy. He hears your prayers, so keep praying. Remember that He may not answer your prayers the way you want or at the time you want, but His grace is always sufficient.

When things in your life do not make sense, keep on praying. Ask God what He wants you to do, and let Him heal you on the inside. He understands that you and I are not perfect. We are works in progress, but we should let Him work within us.

Your peace will come with God's forgiveness and love. Has someone told you that you are unworthy of His love? My first suggestion is to get a second opinion! Ask your heavenly Father to reveal His kindness and love to you. Draw strength from my story if it helps, but know that if you are patient, you will emerge from your despair and find hope.

LIMITLESS *Life*

> You may have difficulty understanding how He can love you. But no matter what you've done in the past, no matter what hurts you have endured, God will heal you with His love if you accept Him. Trust in God so that even if your hardships remain, your mind and heart will be at peace through that season. Again, take it one day at a time, and you will come through these challenges.

30 The Greatest Miracle

> Do not believe me unless I do what my
> Father does. But if I do it, even though you
> do not believe me, believe the miracles, that
> you may know and understand that the
> Father is in me, and I in the Father.
>
> JOHN 10:37–38, NIV

I'm not advising anyone to ever give up hope of healing or change of circumstances. Miracles *can* occur. I've seen many myself, and people often share their own with me. John sent this inspiring story of his miracle, which also offers testimony to his faith in action:

I was not a religious person until about ten years ago when I looked death in the face. When I was young,

I lost my leg due to cancer, and the doctors told me I would not live past five years old, at the very most.

Well, I beat their expectation and on May 6, I turn thirty-seven. But it has not always been easy. The cancer comes out of remission once every several years, and last year it came back harder than ever. My doctors told me that unless I started a rigorous regimen of chemotherapy, I would die within the year.

I immediately shut them down and said I wanted to die and that I was tired of fighting. This cancer has killed my mother, two sisters, and three brothers, so I know it is going to get me someday. I was ready to go!

I spoke with my pastor about my decision, and after a lot of prayer I decided to begin the regimen. I was scheduled two times a week for twelve weeks. Going into my fifth treatment they did blood work and sent the results to my doctor as scheduled. Later that week he called me and asked me to come into the office. When I got there he immediately came into the room and was actually crying. He told me that the cancer was gone! There was no sign of it anywhere. It's like it never existed. He was so happy, but not as much as I was!!

I continue to get checkups every three months, and so far everything is good. I know someday it could come back, and I could even get hit by a bus on the way home from work. The fact is, we never know when our time on this earth will come to an end.

John's story and many others like it that I've heard are proof that miracles can happen. That is why I still keep a pair of shoes in my closet—just in case a miracle comes my way. But if a miracle doesn't come, I can still be a light shining on earth for others.

Can God heal you? Yes, and that may be His plan. Or maybe it isn't. It is impossible to know, so walk in faith every day, knowing that God knows best. I have not received the miracle of arms and legs that I've sought, but I've experienced the miraculous joy and peace and trust of faith. That is more of a miracle than an illness cured. After all, you can be healed of cancer and still be miserable, taking everything in life for granted. By faith today, I honestly have the joy of seeing lives transformed. This is huge! You may rejoice that you have limbs, but each day I rejoice that I do not.

The greatest miracle is transformation from the inside out. The greatest purpose is to know God as a friend and to have the blessing of going home to heaven, where no pain, no sickness, no hardship will ever find you.

I feel badly for those who don't believe in heaven. The thought that we only get one brief shot at life is pretty depressing. I want to live billions of years and into eternity. While I'm in this life, I try to have an impact that will last just as long. It won't matter how much money I've made or how many nice cars I've owned. What will matter is that I've reached out to someone and served a purpose greater than my own.

LIMITLESS *Life*

> All of our names and numbers are in the Book of Life. We just don't know when God will decide to take us home to be with Him. Love each other as if it's your last day on this earth. Live life to the fullest and appreciate every day that you wake up and take a breath.

ACKNOWLEDGMENTS

Most of all, I thank God: Father, Son, and Holy Spirit.

Words cannot express my joy in being able to thank my wife, Kanae, for all the love, care, support, and prayers she gives in abundance to me. I love you, *mi amor*!

I'd like to thank my parents, Boris and Dushka Vujicic, for being such strong pillars of support throughout my life. Thanks, Mum and Dad. My brother, Aaron, the best man at my wedding—thank you and your wife, Michelle, for loving me and keeping me grounded. Michelle, my sister—thanks for believing in me and my dreams. To the new family I now have, the Miyahara and Osuna families; my mother-in-law, Esmeralda; my new brothers, Keisuke, Kenzi, and Abraham; and my new sister, Yoshie—thank you for loving and accepting me into your family.

Thanks again to my relatives and friends who throughout the years have supported me and sown encouragement each step of the way—you all played a part, and I thank you. George Miksa—I pray the Lord continues to carry you and lead you and bless you for helping me start the headquarters of Life Without Limbs in the United States.

Thank you to the board of directors of Life Without Limbs and their families: Batta Vujicic, David Price, Dan'l Markham, Don McMaster, Terry Moore, and Jon Phelps. Thank you, as well, to the advisory board of Life Without Limbs. A very big thank-you to the faithful, diligent, and faith-filled staff of Life Without Limbs. Keep up the great work. Thank you to Ignatius Ho, who helps direct our Hong Kong Life Without Limbs chapter. Thank you to the Apostolic Christian Church of the Nazarene, especially Pasadena, for your support. Thank you also to the Attitude Is Altitude staff and team for backing me, praying for me, and believing with me.

I would like to say a very special thank-you to Wes Smith and his wife, Sarah, for their support. Wes, I could not have asked for a better writing partner. I am very proud of the two books we've written so far.

Thanks once again to my literary agents, Jan Miller Rich and Nena Madonia at Dupree Miller & Associates, who have had faith in me and my purpose from the beginning. Also my deepest thanks to my publisher, WaterBrook Multnomah, a division of Random House, and its sterling team, including Michael Palgon, Gary Jansen, Steve Cobb, and Bruce Nygren, who have encouraged and supported me.

Last, but not less important, thank you to all the people who pray for me, my wife, and our ministry, and to those who financially support us. A big thank-you as well for helping us attain the goals of Life Without Limbs.

Bless all who read this book. I pray that my words open your hearts and minds in a fresh and dynamic way, moving you to put your faith into action while inspiring others to do the same.

What would your life be like if *anything* were possible?

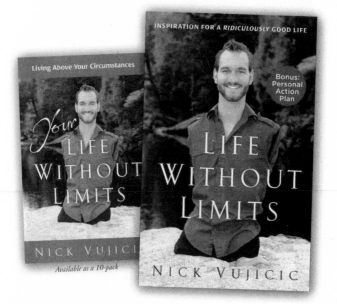

Nick tells the story of his physical disabilities and the emotional battle he endured while learning to deal with them as a child, teen, and young adult. Nick shares how his faith in God has been his major source of strength, and he explains that once he found a sense of purpose—inspiring others to better their lives and the world around them—he found the confidence to build a rewarding and productive life without limits. Let Nick inspire you to start living your own life without limits.

Overcome Your Biggest Obstacles–
whether *emotionally, mentally, spiritually,* or *physically*
–and become
UNSTOPPABLE

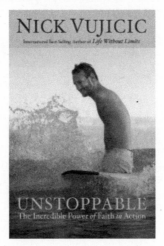

NICK VUJICIC– an internationally-known motivational speaker and evangelist, celebrated for his extraordinary life despite being born limbless – explains in his new book how anyone can release the power to become all they were created to be. Whether it's faith in their purpose, beliefs, talents, creativity, or relationships, all people can take control of their life and achieve their dreams.

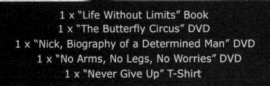